ESTES VALLEY
LIBRARY

# Eyewitness
# Battle

Dutch wheel-lock pistol

Indian spiked mace

British shoulder scales

French footsoldier's backpack

British shoulder belt plate

Italian linstock

Polish or Hungarian war hammer

US Gatling gun

Turkish Order
of Osmanieh

# Eyewitness
# Battle

British
Victoria Cross

Written by
RICHARD HOLMES

Photographed by
GEOFF DANN & GEOFF BRIGHTLING

Swiss
halberd

German
poleax

Indian ax

Indian ax

French shako

DK

DK Publishing

Caucasian pistol

British commemorative
medal

Model of private
of 71st Highland
Light Infantry

German
swept-hilt
rapier

Indian
battle-ax

# DK

## LONDON, NEW YORK,
## MELBOURNE, MUNICH, AND DELHI

**Project editor** Caroline Beattie
**Art editor** Sharon Spencer
**DTP/Design** Ivan Finnegan
**Managing editor** Gillian Denton
**Managing art editor** Julia Harris
**Researcher** Céline Carez
**Production** Catherine Semark
**Picture research** Cynthia Hole

### Revised Edition
**Editors** Jayne Miller, Steve Setford
**Art editors** Edward Kinsey, Peter Radcliffe
**Managing editor** Camilla Hallinan
**Managing art editor** Owen Peyton Jones
**Art director** Martin Wilson
**Associate publisher** Andrew Macintyre
**Production editor** Laragh Kedwell
**Production controller** Pip Tinsley
**Picture research** Myriam Megharbi

This Eyewitness ® Guide has been conceived by
Dorling Kindersley Limited and Editions Gallimard

First published in the United States in 1995
This revised edition published in 2009 by DK Publishing,
375 Hudson Street, New York, New York, 10014

10 11 12 13 10 9 8 7 6 5 4
ED768 – 02/09

A catalog record for this book is available
from the Library of Congress

ISBN 978-0-7566-5027-8 (HC); 978-0-7566-5026-1 (ALB)

Color reproduction by Colourscan, Singapore
Printed by Toppan Co., (Shenzhen) Ltd., China

Discover more at
## www.dk.com

Buttons of the 52nd
Oxfordshire Light
Infantry regiment

British
gorget

# Contents

Japanese Order
of the Rising Sun

# What is battle?

BATTLE IS A CLASH between groups of armed people. It spans most cultures and all continents. Its character—the duration, the number of participants, the weapons, and the tactics employed—is infinitely variable. Battle is intimately bound up with the social, economic, technical, and political features of its age. In the European tradition it was a way for the rulers of one country to force those of another to comply with their wishes. Asian cultures often avoided battle and sought to win by rapid movement or protracted operations. Battle presented many challenges to the courage and resolve of combatants. The German military theorist Carl von Clausewitz (1780–1831) warned that "the character of battle … is slaughter, and its price is blood."

*Original statue would have had spear held in right hand*

**CYPRIOT WARRIORS**
These terra-cotta figurines, made in Cyprus in the seventh century BCE, remind us that a battle is a collective enterprise. The warriors, dressed in armor combining metal plates with fabric, would have held spears and fought in close formation.

*Spear*

*The hoplon gave Greek soldiers the name hoplite*

*Greave being fitted*

*Bronze helmet*

**WARRIORS DRESSING**
The male members of the city-states of ancient Greece had to serve as soldiers when their city went to war. They did military service and kept fit in case they were called up. Greek warriors were armed with a bronze helmet, shin guards called greaves, and each carried a *hoplon*, a heavy shield, on their left arm. They fought in a mass called a phalanx, closely packed together so that the hoplon protected the right side of the man to the left. A long spear was their main weapon.

## FLEEING ARABS

The great battles of history were often short, for the effort of plying a sword or a spear quickly exhausted combatants. Defeated warriors fled and might escape by throwing away their heavy weapons and equipment. Training and discipline were battle-winners. The Assyrians, who lived in the area of modern Iraq in around 1300–600 BCE, were fierce and well organized; these Arabs are fleeing from them.

## CHARGING THE ENEMY

The Egyptians enjoyed a long period of military ascendancy. This wall-painting shows Pharaoh Seti I (ruled 1294–1279 BCE) charging the Libyans in his chariot. War chariots were generally used only by the privileged members of the army.

*Helmet would have been topped by a crest*

## WARRIOR ON HORSEBACK

This bronze statue of a warrior on his horse was made at Taranto in southern Italy in about 550 BCE. The horse was of immense military importance. It helped warriors cover ground quickly on campaign, and in battle, horsemen could ride down unprotected footsoldiers.

*Hands would have held shield and spear*

## A CLASH OF TWO SIDES

Armored knights (the French on the left and the English on the right) at the battle of Poitiers in France in 1356. The physical and psychological demands of combat led to the development of warrior classes, like the European knight and the Japanese samurai, whose very existence was geared to fighting battles.

*Horse and warrior were cast separately*

# Infantry of the line

INFANTRY FORMED THE GREAT MASS of most armies, and unskilled recruits who volunteered for or were conscripted (drafted) into service would usually serve as footsoldiers. In the 18th and 19th centuries, infantry units formed an army's line of battle, so they were called regiments of the line. Regiments were numbered or named after a geographical region; sometimes they were known by the names of their colonels. There were specialized infantry, such as light regiments or rifle regiments, intended for skirmishing, and grenadiers, initially formed to use the hand grenade but later simply elite footsoldiers.

**JOIN UP! JOIN UP!**
Although the Pressing Act of 1704 meant that jobless able-bodied men could be drafted into military service, the British army usually relied on volunteers. A drummer would "beat up" to attract them, and a recruiting sergeant or officer would use cash and promises of regular meals and pay to persuade them to enlist.

**"I WANT YOU FOR THE US ARMY"**
Posters appealed to the patriotic spirit, so as to avoid conscription (forced military service).

**TAKING THE KING'S SHILLING**
Once a man had accepted money from the recruiting sergeant ("taken the king's shilling") by fair means or foul, he was deemed to have enlisted.

*Bayonet*

*National cockade (colored ribbon, here imitated in metal)*

*Shako plate with imperial eagle and regimental number*

**INFANTRY UNIFORM**
This uniform was worn by a corporal of the French 21st Regiment of Infantry in the Napoleonic period. The rank of corporal was indicated by the stripes on the lower sleeve. Infantrymen lived, and often died, on their feet, and so their shoes were heavily studded to help them withstand the rigors of campaigning.

*Chevron on upper sleeve awarded for five years' good conduct*

*Shako*

*Owner's initials*

**REPAIR KIT**
The hussif (derived from the word housewife) was a case for needles, thread, and other bits of sewing equipment. This example was made from pieces of old uniform and embroidered with the owner's regimental colors (pp. 18–19), those of the 93rd Highlanders. It could be rolled up and put in the pack on the march or hung by the soldier's bedside in camp.

*Corporal's stripes*

### AMMUNITION POUCH

This pouch was worn over the left shoulder on its buff leather strap, which incorporated a fitting for the bayonet. It also had a soft cap fastened beneath it.

*This 1777-pattern Charleville musket (pp. 42–43) was the most common weapon of the French infantry*

### SHORT SWORD

The short sword was carried by most Napoleonic French infantrymen. Its value in combat was limited, but it was put to many other uses, such as chopping wood or holding a kettle over the camp fire, in bivouacs (open-air camps).

*Studs helped shoes to last longer*

### DRESSED FOR THE WEATHER

Infantrymen carried warm, long greatcoats that they wore in wet or cold weather. These members of the British 1st Foot Guards are in full marching order (equipment), with packs and cooking utensils on their backs.

### FOOTSOLDIERS

Infantrymen fought on foot. Their uniforms served to clothe and protect them from the weather as well as to give each side a distinctive look—the British are in red and the French are in blue.

*Brass buckle*

### PACK

The Napoleonic infantryman's pack was made from the hide of almost any animal that came to hand, and often had the fur left on to make it more durable. It contained spare clothing and personal effects, and items like a greatcoat or spare shoes could be strapped to the outside.

*Loose-fitting trousers were worn for battle over close-fitting knee breeches*

*Brass buttons embossed with "21," the regimental number*

# Heavy cavalry

FOR MUCH OF HISTORY, cavalry formed two main groups: light cavalry, whose chief tasks were screening (counterreconnaissance), scouting, and the pursuit of a beaten enemy; and heavy cavalry, who were used for shock action (the physical impact of horses and people) on the field of battle. Heavy cavalry, whose function can be traced back to knights, were trained and equipped for the knee-to-knee charge, in which cavalry charged in solid lines. Heavy cavalry were used against both cavalry and infantry. Although it was difficult for even the best cavalry to ride down infantry who stood steady against the onslaught, the thunderous onrush of big men on big horses was very effective and often persuaded shaky infantry to run. Cuirassiers were the classic type of heavy cavalry, whose prestige helped ensure their survival into the early 20th century. A third category of cavalry, dragoons, began as footsoldiers on horseback; they did most of their fighting dismounted, but were eventually regarded as true cavalry.

**CHARGE!**
French cuirassiers charge the Germans in the Franco-Prussian War of 1870–1871. The cuirass alone could weigh as much as 12–15 lb (5.5–6.8 kg).

Snaffle bit

Curb bit

**BIT BETWEEN THE TEETH**
Battles were terrifying both for people and horses, and the simple snaffle bit rarely gave a rider suffcient control of his mount. A harsher curb bit, used with double reins, gave the rider more control.

Stirrups

**VALISE**
A horseman had to carry an assortment of spare clothing and equipment. This valise, its ends decorated with the number of the horseman's regiment, was attached behind the saddle.

**CARBINE**
In 1811, French cuirassiers were issued with carbines. These were shorter than the infantry musket so as to be more handy on horseback, although in practice they were more useful for sentries and outposts than on the battlefield.

*Buckle to attach saddlecloth to saddle*

**SADDLECLOTH**
This saddlecloth was fitted over the horse's hindquarters behind the saddle and under the valise. The grenade badges at its corners symbolize the elite nature of cuirassier regiments. The badge originated with grenadiers, traditionally the biggest and bravest of the infantry, who were trained to throw hand grenades, but it later denoted select troops in general.

**CUIRASS**
The steel of this Napoleonic French cuirassier's breastplate was strong enough to keep out musket balls and sword cuts. It was worn over the uniform jacket and held in place by the shoulder straps and a belt around the waist. The quilted lining protected the wearer from the edges of the metal.

*Backplate*

*Leather shoulder strap, with brass protection*

*Heavy steel, proof against musket balls*

*Breast plate*

*Quilted lining*

*Feather plume for special occasions*

*Horsehair tuft*

*Fur turban*

*Leather chin strap protected by brass scales*

**HELMET**
A man's head presented a vulnerable target. His elaborate helmet had a steel skull, decorated with a fur turban. An embossed brass comb rose above it, with a long horsehair tail falling to the back, partly as ornament and partly to protect his neck. A small horsehair tuft decorated the front of the helmet. The red feather side-plume was initially worn all the time, but in 1808 the 8th Regiment lost 85 in a single day, so plumes were thereafter worn only on special occasions.

*Horsehair "mane"*

**TUNIC AND TROUSERS**
The tunic was made of closely woven material which kept the cold and rain out. The trousers were made of soft white hide, which was comfortable and durable.

*Epaulettes*

*Cuffs decorated with regimental facing colours*

*Cartridge box for ammunition*

*Sword-knot worn around the wrist to keep the sword safe*

**BOOTS**
Heavy leather boots gave some protection against the jostling that went on as men were pressed together in solid lines.

*Brass-hilted sword with a straight, heavy blade; cuirassiers were trained to use the point wherever possible*

# Weapon's training

THE BATTLEFIELD was a terrifying and deadly place. Soldiers had to balance a natural tendency to run away with the desire not to let down comrades and leaders. Soldiers were drilled to make them use their weapons efficiently and to create a cohesive fighting unit with the discipline to withstand the shock of battle. Sometimes courage was promoted by a code of values that dominated an entire social class, like knights in medieval Europe or samurai in feudal Japan. Even so, members of a warrior class still needed training to form efficient armies rather than a collection of individual warriors.

*Stringed bugle badge*

*Plume worn by officers, sergeants, and buglers*

*Cross-belt with whistle for giving orders*

*Backsight: rifles had proper sights, which helped the rifleman aim*

*Officer's sash*

*Sergeant's chevrons*

**READY, AIM, FIRE!**
Some experienced soldiers argued that the aim of drill was to produce unquestioning obedience. Frederick the Great (1713–1786) of Prussia declared that "the common soldier must fear his officer more than the enemy." Others believed in a system founded on two-way trust and respect between officers and men. The British army's rifle regiments obeyed a philosophy that emphasized that "a Corps of Riflemen is expected to be one where intelligence is to distinguish every individual."

*Hilt of sword bayonet*

*Cartridge box contains ammunition*

*Hessian boots (p. 17) worn with spurs by captains and ranks above (these were mounted, even in infantry regiments)*

*Waxed canvas gaiters protect feet in wet weather*

British riflemen demonstrate five different positions for firing the Baker rifle (pp. 42–43)

**HARDEE'S TACTICS**
Drill books were written by officers who hoped to make money or enhance their reputations. These books became especially important when small armies grew rapidly and there were too few trained instructors. Hardee's *Tactics* was widely used by the largely amateur officers during the US Civil War (1861–1865).

**RIFLE DRILL**
Drill books contained plates of soldiers performing the various parts of each drill movement. *The Rifle Manual and Firing Positions* (1804) shows how to "trail arms." In the first part (left) the left hand was brought across the body to seize the rifle level with the shoulder. In the second (center) the right hand moved up to hold the rifle near its point of balance, and in the third (right) the left hand was removed, allowing the rifle to trail on the right side at arm's length.

**SWORD EXERCISES**
It was harder to train a cavalryman than an infantryman, for the former had to be able to ride and look after his horse as well as use his weapons. Cavalrymen, like these troopers, were taught sword drill, which consisted of a number of cuts, points (stabbing movements), and parries (blocking an opponent's sword cuts).

*British rifle regiments wore green rather than the red of the line infantry*

*Sling enabled rifle to be carried over shoulder on march*

*The sitting position was sometimes assumed on hillsides*

Soldiers were taught to march in formation

**13**

*Continued on next page*

# Drill and discipline

Efficient fire and movement depended on slick individual and group drill. Loading and firing drills were especially important, for they could enable one side to fire faster than the other. In the Napoleonic period well-drilled British infantry were able to fire faster than their opponents. Good drill also helped to prevent accidents: Marshal Gouvion St.-Cyr (1764–1830) estimated that one-quarter of French infantry casualties in the Napoleonic period were caused by soldiers being accidentally shot by men behind them. Drill, and emphasis on smartness and cleanliness also helped to create a climate of disciplined obedience, in which the soldier would carry out orders instinctively. Finally, snappy drill and smart uniforms fostered a soldier's self-esteem, giving him pride and confidence in himself and his unit.

*Hole for buttons*

*Button of 52nd Oxfordshire Regiment (Light Infantry)*

*Name of owner's regiment*

*Regimental battle honor for the 1801 Egyptian campaign*

**MIGHTY RULER**
Genghis Khan (1162–1227) led Mongol armies over huge tracts of Central Asia, China, and Russia. He was a skilled general and administrator, and his armies were not the undisciplined hordes of popular mythology, but well-organized bands of horsemen.

**GEAR INSPECTION**
This scene in a British 19th-century barracks would have been familiar to soldiers in most armies. Soldiers laid all their belongings out in a set manner ready for inspection. The officer would check that all items were present, clean, and in good condition.

**BRIGHT AS A BUTTON**
In peacetime, much time was devoted to keeping uniform and equipment clean and neat. Brass buttons had to be polished daily, and to keep the polish from staining the tunic, the soldier used a button stick. The buttons were inserted through the hole and then slid down the slot so that several could be polished at once.

*Markers and guides helped soldiers keep in straight lines*

*Color party (regimental colors and escort)*

*Lieutenant-colonel (commanding officer)*

*Sergeant major*

*Junior major commands left wing of battalion*

*Adjutant (commanding officer's personal staff officer)*

**DRILL BLOCKS**
Officers needed to know how to drill large bodies of men so that they could move companies (about 100 men) and battalions (about 800 men) from the column of march to the line of battle and not get them tangled up ("clubbed"). These military drill blocks, each of which represents an individual or a small group of men, enabled officers to practice drawing up units in various formations.

### ADVANCING IN A LINE
These soldiers were trained to march in a straight line in order to use their weapons effectively. They gained reassurance from the presence of comrades to the left and right and brave leadership by officers. The Scots Fusilier Guards (as they were then known) advancing toward the Russians at the Battle of the Alma (Crimean War, 1854–1856).

*Front rank of company*

*Rear rank of company*

A battalion drawn up in line, in six companies, each of two ranks

*Captain commands company*

*Senior major commands right wing of battalion*

### FORMING A SQUARE
There were times when drill was a matter of life and death. Infantrymen in a line were able to deliver the maximum volume of fire, but they were vulnerable to attack by charging cavalry. To meet this threat they formed squares, which were almost invulnerable to cavalry. The drill for forming a square had to be performed quickly and without fuss.

*Hinge, held by sergeant or sergeant major when stick was in use*

*Brass bar for adjusting size of pace*

### PACING IT OUT
To ensure that soldiers moved at the same speed, they were trained to take paces of uniform length and to take a set number of paces a minute. This pace stick, really a giant pair of dividers, is still used in the British army for measuring the length of paces.

*Polished wood*

*End tipped with brass to make it more durable*

# Badges of rank

Shoulder cord worn by a field marshal

Shoulder cord worn by a colonel

Shoulder cord worn by a captain

ARMIES ARE LARGE and complex organizations and can only be run efficiently if they have a clear chain of command. Badges of rank enabled status to be recognized easily. They also helped to reinforce the military spirit by creating a climate of discipline and formality. There were many ways of indicating rank, such as the carrying of specific weapons or the wearing of more elaborate clothing by senior personnel. In the Chinese army, for example, the senior mandarins wore tunics embroidered with particular symbols to denote their rank. Gradually, in the 19th century, most armies around the world turned to indicating rank by distinctive badges worn on the sleeve, collar, or epaulette.

**ZULU ARMY**
In the Zulu army, officers were distinguished by leopard-skin kilts or capes and by certain types of blue feather. Although in the 18th century regiments were uniformly dressed, by the end of the 19th century members of inexperienced regiments carried black shields that they exchanged for white ones as their regiment's reputation grew.

Badge of a warrant officer class 1, worn on cuff

NCO's chevrons (sergeant), worn on sleeve

NCO's chevrons (corporal), worn on sleeve

**BRITISH BADGES**
Most armies make a distinction between commissioned officers, who hold a commission signed by the head of state or commander-in-chief; warrant officers, whose warrant of appointment carries a more junior status; and non-commissioned officers (NCOs), who can be appointed more easily. Over the past century, badges of rank worn on field uniforms have become increasingly inconspicuous to prevent leaders from being singled out by enemy marksmen.

*Parchment leaf*

**JAPANESE FAN**
The war fan was carried by Japanese officers in the time of the samurai as a mark of their rank. It could be used for signaling and, when closed, could parry a sword cut or club an opponent. The fan itself was usually made of iron covered with parchment decorated with the Sun of Japan.

*Iron sticks*

**THE THIN RED LINE**
During the Crimean War battle of Balaclava (1854), Russian cavalry threatened the British base in Balaclava itself. The attack was thwarted by the "Thin Red Line" of the 93rd Sutherland Highlanders. The officer directing the fire shows his rank by wearing a sash and epaulettes and by carrying a sword. There is a corporal, with two chevrons, in the front rank, and a sergeant, with three chevrons, to the rear.

## INDIAN CHIEF
The elaborate feather headdress of this North American Plains Indian chief signifies, to friends and enemies alike, that he is a man of importance.

*Hat worn in battle with removable cover; on parade, it was worn without the cover and with a plume*

Officer's epaulette worn on the shoulders of full dress uniform

*Gilt epaulette with bullion fringes*

*Gorget*

*Shoulder belt holds sword*

## OFFICER'S DRESS
This uniform of a British officer in the 7th Royal Fusiliers would have been worn on active service in the period 1802–10. Officer status is shown by the cut and quality of the uniform, its gold lace, the gorget at the neck, the waist sash, and the 1796-pattern sword. Specific ranks were indicated by the epaulettes, which were gilt (metal covered with gold).

Officer's shoulder scale worn on the shoulders of undress uniform

## ON THE SHOULDER
Epaulettes were worn on either one or both shoulders to denote officers of different ranks.

*Leather pouch contains telescope*

*Strap worn across shoulder*

*Silk sash*

Epaulette worn by supply officer

*Officer's sword*

## BATON
This French or Italian commander's baton from around 1700 is a fine example of an item which long symbolized high command. It was said that the French Napoleonic soldier, who might gain promotion regardless of social origins, "had a marshal's baton in his knapsack." British field marshals still carry batons on ceremonial occasions.

*Leather Hessian boots, originally from Hesse in Germany*

## GORGET
The gorget, worn in the British army until 1830 as the symbol of an officer on duty, began as a piece of armor that protected the throat.

# Regimental colors

Like the eagles carried by Roman legions and the banners of medieval nobles, colors had both symbolic and practical importance. Symbolically, colors were the soul of a regiment: their loss in battle was a matter of deep disgrace. A British officer, whose regiment was in a desperate plight at Waterloo, felt relieved when he saw the "dear old rags" marched off to safety. Practically, they enabled soldiers to recognize their units and rally to them in the confusion of battle. The color was regularly trooped through the ranks of a regiment so that men would recognize it.

**COATS OF ARMS**
Early colors often had items from the commanding officer's coat of arms. This shield, carried by King Matthias Corvinus of Hungary and Bohemia (around 1443–1490), bears his arms.

**BATTLE HONORS**
Glorious past achievements were marked in many ways. This British shabraque (officer's horse blanket) is embroidered with battle honors for Dettingen (1743), the Peninsular War (1808–1814), Waterloo (1815), Egypt (1882), and Tel el Kebir (1882).

**COLOR PARTY**
The regimental color of the 9th East Norfolk Regiment is carried by an ensign, the most junior rank of commissioned officer, whose title is itself another word for flag. Behind him a color sergeant uses his short pike to defend the color. Ensigns were usually very young and in close-quarter battle relied heavily on their color sergeants to defend them.

*Silk matches facings (collars and cuffs) on uniforms*

*Colors normally supported in this belt*

**HUSSAR STANDARD**
French hussar standard, from the time of the republic in the late 18th century. This republican pattern was replaced by one with Napoleonic eagles. Hussars and other light cavalry, whose tasks demanded risk and isolation, did not always carry standards.

**CHINESE COLORS**
Here a Japanese officer is in the act of capturing a Chinese flag in the Sino-Japanese war over Korea (1894–1895). The symbolism of colors was international.

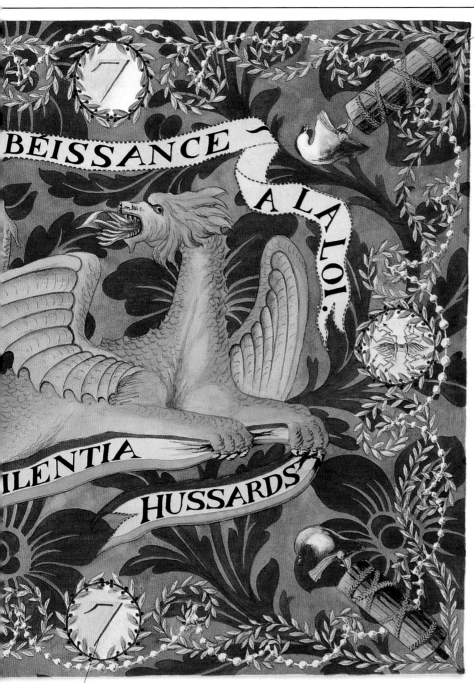

BÉISSANCE A LA LOI.

...ILENTIA HUSSARDS

*Symbol of unity*

*Eagle held thunderbolt as a symbol of power*

**EAGLE**
The Emperor Napoleon introduced the eagle as France's national symbol, and the eagles carried by French regiments consciously harkened back to those of the Roman legions. This eagle of the French 105th Regiment of the Line was lost to the British at Waterloo in 1815.

**FIGHT FOR THE STANDARD**
Regimental colors inevitably became the center of fierce fighting as attackers sought to seize them from their bearers. Here Union and Confederate cavalrymen struggle for possession of a Confederate standard during the Civil War (1861–1865). Men often risked their lives to protect their colors: at the Battle of Rezonville (Franco-Prussian War, 1870–1871), the colors of the French 3rd Grenadiers of the Guard were passed from hand to hand as successive bearers were shot down. Eventually the regimental commander died waving them and shouting "To the color, my boys."

*Number indicates 7th Hussars*

*Regimental symbols embroidered on silk ground*

*Latin inscription meaning "Second to None," a pun on the regimental number*

**CAVALRY COLORS**
Guidon of the 3rd Troop, 2nd Royal North British Dragoons, about 1780. This swallow-tailed guidon is typical of cavalry standards. For many years colors were carried by individual infantry companies or cavalry troops, but the practice generally died out in the 18th century.

# Supply and transportation

Logistics is the practical art of moving an army and keeping it supplied: there is considerable truth in the saying that "Amateurs talk tactics while professionals talk logistics." Until World War I, food for men and horses was an army's main requirements. Many commanders tried to "live off the country" by obtaining food from areas they crossed. But even the small armies of medieval Europe (some as small as 8,000 men) found this difficult. Armies also needed large numbers of horses. In 1700 an army of 60,000 men would have had about 40,000 horses. These would eat 550 tons (500 metric tons) of fodder a day. Inventions like the steam-driven train, gas-powered truck, and canned food made things simpler, but at the same time improvements in weaponry increased the burden: by 1916 a British infantry division needed 20 railroad cars of food and 30 of ammunition every day.

**INDIAN CAVALRY**
Asian commanders, facing inhospitable terrain and distances that dwarfed those in Europe, needed a firm grasp on logistics. The horse armies of antiquity—like the Magyars of Hungary, the Seljuk Turks, and the Mongols—were masters of rapid movement. These 18th-century cavalrymen from the northwest Indian state of Jaipur have bags of provisions hanging from their camels.

**FRENCH TROOPS ENTRAINING**
The railroad revolutionized war, enabling huge armies to be moved quickly and in a more organized way, with fewer accidents or desertions. In addition, soldiers and horses would be rested and fit to fight on arrival at the battlefield. In the Austro-Prussian War of 1866, the Prussians sent 200,000 men to the frontier with astonishing speed. In World War I (1914–1918), so many of the Frenchmen who went to war by train in 1914 did not return that it was said that they had been "eaten by the Gare de l'Est" (a large station in Paris).

**THE RUSSIAN RAILROAD**
The railroad was very valuable to large nations, or ones that, like Germany in World War I, had to face enemies on two sides. These Cossacks are being transported eastward on the Trans-Siberian Railroad to reinforce the Russian army fighting the Japanese in Manchuria during the Russo-Japanese War of 1904–1905.

**SOYER OVEN**
British army food was almost inedible during the Crimean War (1853–1856). The great chef Alexis Soyer (1809–1858) went out to help improve cooking. Here he is shown (on the left of the central group) with one of his specially designed ovens behind him.

Saxon baggage wagon, used to transport provisions or camping equipment

*Pair of horses attached here*

**BIVOUAC IN SPAIN**
Moving armies could either be billeted (lodged with local inhabitants) or could bivouac, or camp, in improvised open-air encampments. Bivouacking was essential in sparsely populated areas and was a way of keeping men under better control. Here, British soldiers are setting up a bivouac in Spain during the Peninsular War (1808–1814).

*Lid lifts to give access to baggage*

*Large wheels were better on poor roads*

**TRAVELING FORGE**
Horses required new horseshoes at regular intervals: in August 1914 one of the five German armies in France had 84,000 horses. This traveling forge was kept going on the line of march, enabling blacksmiths to shoe horses or repair metalwork.

*Part attached to horse*

*Bellows to fan fire*

*Coals kept hot by being blown by bellows*

**FRENCH *VIVANDIERE***
Civilian merchants provided armies with many of their needs. French regiments had uniformed *vivandières* to sell comforts like nips of brandy. This cartoon from the Crimean War shows a *vivandière* mocking the Russians.

**SAXON BAGGAGE WAGON**
Until transportation services became organized as a uniformed branch of the army in the 19th century, armies supplemented their own wagons with civilian vehicles and drivers when war broke out. This led to difficulties as drivers deserted and wagons broke down. Wagons built for military purposes were robust; this one was also small enough to be moved by soldiers if necessary. This wagon was used by the Saxon army in the late 18th century.

# A soldier's pack

A SOLDIER'S LIFE ON THE ROAD involved weeks, sometimes months, of carrying spare clothing, water, cooking equipment, tools, and ammunition. Because stocking up on supplies was not always convenient, each man was responsible for carrying his own things for the duration of a campaign; experienced soldiers tended to jettison nonessential items. Equipment was often designed so that items not required in battle were kept in a backpack that could be removed before action, but this was not ideal because the victor would have to pause to recover his pack and the vanquished might lose his altogether.

*Wool cloak*

*Mattock for digging ditches*

*Pack for personal items and three days' rations*

*Leather bottle for water or wine*

**ROMAN SOLDIER**
A fully loaded legionary marched with a pack on his back in addition to his helmet, armor, shield, and weapons. The burden weighed 90 lb (40 kg) or more and might have had to be carried up to 20 miles (32 km) a day.

*Turf cutter for building turf ramparts*

*Shaft of javelin*

*String was doused with water to keep contents cool*

A soldier's water bottle, which stayed with him throughout his service

**A PACK UNPACKED**
Much of what a soldier carried, like spare clothing and cooking utensils, was government issue. A change of clothes called fatigues was included, and they were worn when off duty and for doing fatigues (chores) such as cleaning the mess. Many personal items, such as a razor and a shaving brush, were bought privately. No seasoned soldier wished to carry more than was necessary, but "home comforts" could make all the difference on campaigns in inhospitable places.

Camp kettle, used as a cooking pot as well as a plate

Bill hook for cutting food and chopping firewood

Shoe brush

Badger-hair shaving brush

Fork, knife, and spoon

Straight razor

Shaving bowl

Clothes brush

Soap

Tin mug

**COMPACT PACK**
As well as his pack, this rifleman carries a cartridge box for his ammunition, a white bag for his bread ration, a water bottle, and his rifle.

*Brass buckle did not rust in rain*

*Stitched leather strip holds pack lid together*

**DIG IN THE BACK**
The Trotter back-pack was supported by a rigid wooden frame. It was so uncomfortable on long marches that soldiers often threw away the frame altogether.

Trotter backpack used by armies fighting during the Napoleonic Wars (1799–1815)

*Wool blanket unrolled to keep soldier warm on march and in camp*

A Scottish soldier in full equipment—"marching order"—in 1815

*Tough canvas flaps are folded over to protect contents of pack*

*Jacket was made of comfortable, durable cotton*

# Reconnaissance

*Emblem of French 8th Hussars*

**SABRETACHE**
It is not easy for someone on a horse to keep writing materials accessible yet protected from the weather. So soldiers on reconnaissance, as well as others, wore a sabretache, which was in effect a field writing case. Inside it were compartments for pens, ink, and writing paper. The outer flap was usually decorated.

*Sabretache hung on sword belt*

THE DUKE OF WELLINGTON (1769–1852), a British military commander, declared that the business of war consisted of finding out "what you don't know from what you do." Reconnaissance (surveying an area to gather information) is of fundamental importance, for without it commanders cannot know the strength or location of hostile forces or the nature of the ground they wish to cross. They risk being taken by surprise or advancing into country where an army will find it hard to move or to sustain itself. For centuries light cavalry, riding out ahead of the advancing columns, was the main means of reconnaissance, although it was also done on foot. With the development first of balloons and then aircraft, the "cavalry of the clouds" assumed growing importance, but even in the 21st century a mix of air and ground reconnaissance works best.

**COMPASS**
This compass could be used both for verifying the direction of a march and for finding out the geographical location of distant places such as a house or a hill.

*Lid to protect inner glass*

*Glass cover*

*Needle moves to show North*

**SKETCH**
This sketch map of the fortifications of Savannah, Georgia, was made by a Swiss officer in the British service during the Revolutionary War (1775–1783). Officers needed to make an accurate record of information they acquired, and field sketching was widely taught at military academies.

*Road to Cherokee Hill*

*Town*
*18th Sept.*

*River Savannah*

*Battery position for four guns*

*Lines show steep slope*

**TELESCOPE**
For centuries commanders used the "perspective glass" (telescope) to observe enemy positions. This is a signaler's telescope, which enabled its user to read flag or light signals in the distance.

*Telescope retracts for storage*

A view of the Battle of Fleurus
painted on the lid of a snuff box

## OBSERVATION BALLOON

On June 26, 1794, a French army met an allied Austro-German army at Fleurus, in Belgium. The French sent up a balloon, named *L'Entreprenant*, to hang over the battlefield, and observers sent messages sliding down its rope. However, these were of little value, and although the French won the battle, observation balloons fell out of favor until the Civil War (1861–1865).

## RECONNAISSANCE AIRCRAFT

Military aircraft made their debut in 1911 when the Italians flew reconnaissance missions against the Turkish in Tripolitania (in Libya) and dropped some small bombs. Although air reconnaissance provided good information, pilots ran the risk of being shot down once they had been seen.

*Strap to hang binoculars around neck when in use*

## BROADER VIEW

Originally made from two telescopes joined together, binoculars were easier to use than a telescope. Although they did not usually produce the same degree of magnification, they generally gave a broader field of view. This pair of binoculars was presented by one officer to another officer who had saved his life.

*Case to protect lenses when binoculars were not in use*

## HUSSAR PATROL

These British hussars of 1811 are typical of the light cavalry who played a key role in reconnaissance. They had to move discreetly to keep from being seen or heard by the enemy.

# Field guns

FOR MUCH OF HISTORY, cannon were muzzleloaders (front-loading), firing solid cannonballs at a target well within view. Artillery emerged as the main casualty-producer of 20th-century battles. But this was only after technological advances, mostly in the 19th century, had produced breechloading (rear-loading) weapons whose explosive shells were more deadly than either the roundshot or primitive shells filled with black powder used by earlier guns.

*Seats for gunners*    *Muzzle*

*Footrest*    *Bucket*

### CANNON
This British six-pounder of the mid-19th century shows the muzzleloading cannon at its peak. Its crew of five could fire a 6-lb (2.7-kg) ball to a maximum range of 3,300 feet (1,000 m) two or three times a minute.

*Couplings attached the harnessed horses to the limber*

*Tools are stored on the back of the limber*

*Explosive shells*

*Fuse to explode shell*

*Bags containing gunpowder*

*Cannon attached to limber during transport*

*Ammunition chests are safely locked during transport*

### LIMBER
The cannon was towed directly behind its limber, whose chest contained sufficient ammunition to keep the gun supplied for some time. Ammunition wagons (caissons) would be used to replenish limbers if ammunition ran short. The limber also carried tools to help the detachment to prepare the gun's position. The six-horse team pulling this gun was attached to the couplings.

### ASSEMBLING
When mounting a gun, the barrel required skilled handling. That of a light six-pounder weighed 670 lb (305 kg).

### EARLY CANNONS
Simple cannons from around 1400 caused few casualties but could terrify both horses and new soldiers.

### FUENTES DE ONORO
Horse artillery, with all gunners on horseback, was intended to keep pace with cavalry. At the Battle of Fuentes de Oñoro (Spain, 1811) an English horse artillery battery was surrounded by French cavalry, but the English charged right through the enemy horsemen to escape.

*Elevating wheel for elevating (raising) and depressing (lowering) the barrel*

*Worm for extracting unfired charge from gunbarrel*

*Portfire cutter*

**READY TO MOVE**
When the gun had been coupled up with its limber—had been "limbered up"—it was ready to be moved, by horses or by gunners where necessary.

*Trunnions, on which the barrel pivoted*

*Portfire*

**LINSTOCK**
The linstock, with a smouldering cord in it jaws, was one means of firing the cannon. It was mounted on a pole, enabling the firer to stand clear of the gun as it recoiled (rolled back after firing). It could also be used to light a faster-burning portfire.

*Gunpowder and then a cannon-ball were pushed into the muzzle*

*A lighted linstock or portfire is applied to the touchhole (also called the vent) to fire the cannon*

*Barrel*

*Gunners rode on these seats when the gun was on the move*

**DISASSEMBLING**
Gunners spent long hours perfecting their drills. These included not only loading and firing, but also dismounting and mounting the gun so they could replace damaged parts speedily.

**CUIRASS**
This cuirass was worn by a French soldier in a regiment of *carabiniers* (heavy cavalry). He was killed at the battle of Waterloo (Belgium, 1815), probably during one of the massed cavalry charges against the Duke of Wellington's defensive line, by a small cannonball that smashed right through his protective armor.

*Continued on next page*

# Serving the guns

The detachment of men who operated cannons and mortars needed to be expert at drills for loading and firing. Good drills helped men to keep up a rapid rate of fire, avoid mistakes, and remain effective despite enemy fire. Muzzleloading cannon were loaded with gunpowder, usually in bagged charges. The bag was rammed home and followed with a projectile, which could be a solid ball, explosive shell, or some form of multiple shot. Early cannons were fired by lighting fine priming powder sprinkled into the touchhole. Later, a friction primer was inserted into the vent and fired by pulling a cord called a lanyard.

*Worm*

*Brush for swabbing out the barrel*

*Arms can be straightened out to make a ruler*

*Ball fits into arms of callipers so that weight can be read off calibrations*

**CALLIPERS**
For many years there was no proper standardization of cannons or their projectiles, and gunners needed to be sure that ammunition was the right size. A cannonball had to be a snug fit, with just a little gap (known as windage) between it and the barrel. Gunners used callipers like these to measure cannonballs.

*Slow-burning cord*

*Portfire*

*Clamp to hold portfire*

**RAMMER**
The rammer was used to ram the gunpowder charge and the shot into the barrel. Its staff was made of a tough wood such as hickory.

**WORM**
Sometimes gunners needed to unload their cannon without firing it, or replace one kind of projectile with another. The worm was twisted into the barrel to hook the charge bags in order to withdraw them.

**LINSTOCK**
A linstock had a length of slow-match held in its jaws, which burned at the rate of 40 in (1 m) in about eight hours. It was used to light the portfire.

**PORTFIRE**
The portfire was lit with the linstock and was used to light the cannon. This portfire had a wooden holder with a length of quick burner attached to it, which burned at the rate of 1 in (2.5 cm) per minute. It was lit to fire the cannon and extinguished immediately afterward.

*End used for ramming*

*Spike to stick linstock in ground*

*Portfire holder*

**PART OF THE CREW**
Molly Pitcher (1744–1832), a legendary heroine of the Revolutionary War, had been taking water to men in battle when her husband was killed at his gun. She took his place and we see her ramming while one gunner lays (aims) the gun, and another, acting on his instructions, uses handspikes to swing the weapon around.

**FLAMING SHOT**
Although solid shot was most common, other projectiles were available. This experimental roundshot was intended to have inflammable material in it to set fire to buildings, for example.

**GRAPESHOT**
Multiple shot, such as grapeshot, shown here, or canister (a container of musket balls), split up on leaving the gun's muzzle. It was murderous at close range.

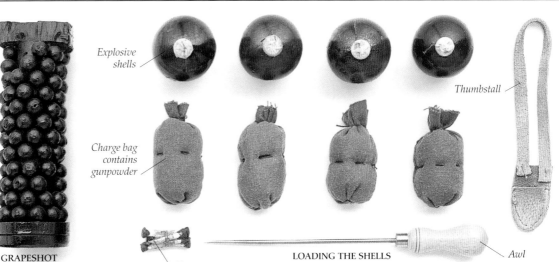

*Explosive shells*

*Thumbstall*

*Charge bag contains gunpowder*

*Fuses*

*Awl*

**LOADING THE SHELLS**
A bag full of powder was loaded, followed by a solid shot or an explosive shell. A long awl was thrust through the vent to enable a fuse or fine priming powder to enter the bagged charge. The thumbstall was held over the vent when a gun was swabbed out after firing, to prevent a draft that might light smouldering debris left by the charge bag.

**TAKE YOUR PICK**
An assortment of tools was carried, usually on the cannon's limber. The pick enabled gunners to break up the ground when they needed to.

**THE LAST CANNON**
British gunners are here shown firing one of the last muzzleloading cannons in British service. Breech-loading cannons were successfully used by the Germans in the Franco-Prussian War (1870–1871), and most other nations soon introduced them. The gunners stood clear to avoid injury when the gun jumped back on recoil.

**SHOVEL**
If gunners had time, they could make their task easier by sloping the ground beneath the gun so that it would naturally roll back into the firing position after recoil.

**ESSENTIAL AX**
The ax enabled gunners to cut away roots or branches in the way.

**BUCKET FOR THE BARREL**
Water was essential for loading, since gunners needed to swab the barrel after firing to ensure that no sparks remained to ignite the next powder charge inserted, and to help remove fouling (the remnants of burned powder).

# Rapid-fire weapons

TRADITIONAL WEAPONS had to be laboriously loaded each time they were fired, so inventors experimented with multibarreled guns to increase the rate of fire. However, it was not until the mid-19th century that good rapid-fire weapons were produced. The Gatling gun, patented by Dr. Richard Gatling (1818–1903), had a number of barrels, most often 10. As they were cranked around by hand, each was fed with a cartridge and fired. A few Gatling guns saw service in the Civil War (1861–1865), but the weapon was used throughout the world by the 1870s. The French army adopted the mitrailleuse in 1865. Its barrels remained stationary. A plate filled with ammunition was inserted into the breech, and the operator turned the firing crank to fire each barrel in turn.

**MITRAILLEUSE**
The mitrailleuse, whose name literally means "grapeshot shooter," had a maximum effective range of 1,650 yards (1,500 m) against a large target. A gunner inserts a loaded plate.

**AMMUNITION**
The development of cartridges whose gunpowder was contained in sturdy brass or copper cases made possible the development of rapid-fire weapons. Both the mitrailleuse and the Gatling gun could fire special cartridges containing several bullets. Shown above is a buckshot round for the Gatling.

*Crank to turn barrels*

*Magazine contained cartridges and fed them into the barrel as they were needed*

*Barrel*

*Crank*

*Ammunition fired from these holes*

*Elevating gear for elevating (raising) and depressing (lowering) the barrels*

**THE GATLING GUN**
Early machine guns were mounted on carriages like conventional field guns. This encouraged officers to regard them as a type of artillery, or to consider them as special weapons for the defence of streets or bridges, because they were heavy and difficult to move. It was not until they were lighter and mounted on tripods (bottom right) that their real potential as infantry weapons emerged.

*Axle*

*Ring to take handspike to swing gun left and right*

*Trail enabled the gun to be towed and provided a prop when it was in use*

*Magazine with ammunition; this version of the Gatling, used by the British in India and Africa, took 1-in- (2.5-cm-) caliber cartidges*

## FRANCO-PRUSSIAN WAR

In the Franco-Prussian War of 1870–1871 the French failed to use the mitrailleuse to its best effect, keeping it back with the field guns, rather than pushing it forward with the infantry. As a consequence, it was usually knocked out by superior German cannons. Because development had been secret, few officers and men knew how it worked, and its mechanism was so fragile that untrained men often broke it.

*Foresight*

*Pivot for revolving mechanism*

*Barrels*

## THE BUSINESS END

Gatling guns were made in several calibers between ½ in (1 cm) and 1 in (2.5 cm). Most had ten barrels, which could be cranked fast enough to fire more than 1,000 rounds a minute.

Dr. Gatling in 1893, with his light gun equipped with a drum magazine

*Shackle for attaching rope helped gunners move gun on difficult ground*

# High-angle fire

**FIRING UP**
The gunner fires an explosive bomb from his mortar over fortifications. Cannons and mortars between them caused a revolution in fortress design. The high stone walls that had characterized medieval fortification offered easy targets. They were replaced by low, squat "artillery fortifications" that were much harder to damage. Important buildings, like ammunition warehouses, were built with strong roofs covered with dirt to make them "bomb-proof"—able to resist mortar bombs.

A CANNON REACHES MAXIMUM RANGE with its barrel at an angle of 45 degrees. Above this level the weapon is said to be firing at a high angle; low-angle fire is below 45 degrees. Mortars were short and stubby and were specifically designed for high-angle fire. They fired bombs (explosive shells) when most guns fired only solid balls, and they were used in sieges because their projectiles would pass over fortifications to burst inside the town or fortress. Howitzers were longer-barreled and could fire at low or high angles. Like mortars, they used shells when these were uncommon in cannons. Mortars and howitzers remained important because they could fire over ridges and drop shells into sheltered ground or trench systems. Small "trench mortars" were widely used in World War I (1914–1918).

**LOW-ANGLE FIRE**
This gunner is using low-angle fire, sending a solid cannonball against fortifications or troops. His cannon is protected by gabions (wicker baskets filled with dirt).

**GUNNER LIGHTING FUSE**
Early mortars required "double ignition." The gunner would first light the fuse on the bomb, and then fire the mortar. This was a dangerous practice: sometimes the mortar failed to fire and its bomb exploded in the barrel, causing casualties and damage. It was later discovered that the flash of the mortar being fired would also ignite the fuse on the bomb.

*Royal emblem*

*Bed*

*Carrying handle*

**COEHOORN MORTAR**
Not all mortars were heavy. The engineer Menno van Coehoorn (1641–1704), known as "The Dutch Vauban" (pp. 54–55), designed a light mortar that could be manhandled around fortifications or even taken into the field. The Coehoorn mortar was used by many armies and remained in service until the end of the Civil War (1861–1865).

Winch used to
lift heavy bomb
and lower it
into the muzzle

13-inch
mortar
bomb

## SHELL
Common shell consisted of a
hollow iron shell filled with
powder. A fuse would ignite the
powder to burst the shell,
fragmenting the case, which would
cause casualties and damage.

Fuse

Powder

## SHRAPNEL
Spherical case shot was often known
as shrapnel, after Lieutenant Henry
Shrapnel, who designed a version in
1784. It was intended to burst in the
air, scattering balls onto the target.

Fuse

Balls set in
charge of
gunpowder
to burst
the shell

Handle to wind
winch cord up
and down

Big muzzle
enabled big
bombs to
be fired

Handles were called
dolphins because they
were traditionally
made in that shape

## HOWITZER
Heavy howitzers were used to attack or defend fortifications, and
for coastal defense. This mid-19th-century French howitzer used 55
lb (25 kg) of powder to fire a 550-lb (250-kg) shell. Two gunners
are at work on the hoist, hauling a powder charge up for loading.

## PROTOTYPE MORTAR
The 13-inch (33-cm) mortar, in use
from around 1760 to about 1860,
was the largest in the British service.
Its barrel weighed 2,800 lb (1,270 kg)
and its wooden bed over 2,350 lb
(1,067 kg). This prototype is mounted
on an even heavier brass bed. It would
have formed part of a siege train (an
assembly of siege guns), brought up
to mount a siege.

## US MORTAR BATTERY
During the Civil War the Union army
besieged Yorktown, establishing
batteries to bombard the town. This
photograph shows battery No. 4,
equipped with mortars.

Brass bed

# Artillery instruments

EARLY CANNONS WERE CUMBERSOME and inaccurate. Prussian gunners maintained that "the first shot is for God, the second is for the devil, and only the third is for the king." In the earliest textbook on gunnery (1537) Niccolo Tartaglia described the relationship between the speed of the cannonball and the path it followed, writing "the more swift the pellet doth fly, the less crooked is its range." To make the most of their cannon, gunners needed instruments to position them correctly. They used quadrants to find the angle of elevation and calculate how far a shot would go. Rules enabled them to measure a cannon's muzzle to establish the weight of ball it fired, levels helped them to place guns precisely upright, and they used dividers to measure ranges on maps.

*Pendulum to ensure that level is upright*

Gunner's quadrant, placed against underside of mortar barrel to measure its angle

**GUNNER'S LEVEL**
This level was shaped to stand on the breech of a cannon: when the pendulum was central, the gun was standing level.

**VENT CLEANERS**
Instruments of this kind often fit in the scabbard of the elaborate sword sometimes carried by master gunners.

*Studs protect the pole from wear, as well as holding the quadrant in place*

*Label shows which kind of shot the scale is for—in this case, gravel*

SLAG

**QUADRANT IN USE**
A gunner would slide the quadrant down the barrel of the gun, and then read off the angle of elevation indicated by the plumb line.

**UP, UP, AND AWAY!**
This fanciful engraving of 1789 shows a mortar firing a large bomb and several smaller ones. Mortars could fire multiple projectiles, but these were usually the same size, and it was difficult to ensure that all ignited properly.

## MORTARS

Mortars fired explosive projectiles in a high-angled trajectory (above 45 degrees), usually at a target behind town walls. Gunners would know at what angle the gun barrel needed to be so that a particular cannonball would reach a particular target. This German engraving of 1575 shows two mortars on their carriages, with a gunner's quadrant in the right foreground.

*Intricate decoration shows that these were precious instruments*

*Pendulum to ensure that level is upright*

*Scale of degrees*

Gunner's protractor to measure angle of gun barrel

Dividers for measuring distances on maps

*Leg can be replaced by blade, pen, or pencil*

Compasses

*Point to clear out vent before inserting powder*

*Screw for loosening powder encrusted in a cannon's vent*

Gunner's rule

## GUNNER'S RULES

A gunner would place a rule across the mouth of a cannon and read off a measurement. This would tell him the weight of shot to use. Each side of the rule was calibrated for a different type of shot (stone or lead, for example).

*Coat of arms*

*Pendulum*

## GUNNER'S QUADRANT

This instrument, a gunner's quadrant, was made in Germany in 1585. Its scales gave the angles of elevation and depression of a gun barrel. It could also measure the angle to a target: the gunner looked through the eyepiece, along the staff, and read the angle off the quadrant. Each edge of the staff has measurements for different types of shot—stone, iron, or lead balls, and *slaggen* (gravel), a primitive but unpleasant projectile.

# Bows and arrows

**W**EAPONS THAT WERE SHOT and thrown enabled their users to attack an opponent from a distance. Bows played a major role in battle. The longbow, made of wood or a combination of materials like wood and horn, was deadly in skilled hands and could even send its arrow through some types of armor. However, it took years of practice to use one effectively. The crossbow was more powerful than the longbow, but was heavier and had a slower rate of fire. Both longbow and crossbow were used in medieval Europe. Thrown weapons, including javelins (throwing spears), were used by people all over the world, such as Romans, African peoples, and Aboriginal Australians. Hand grenades came into use in the 17th century and did more damage than other thrown weapons by exploding on impact.

**FIREWORKS**
Arrows tipped with inflammable compounds could be shot into wooden buildings or on to thatched roofs to cause fires. These 17th-century illustrations (above and right) show slightly fanciful versions of flaming arrows.

*Armor-piercing bodkin point*

*Gap in arrowhead made it lighter*

*Painted, gilt, and lacquered decoration*

*Barb*

*Strong, flexible bamboo shaft*

*Thickened tip for piercing light armor*

**INDIAN ARROWS**
An archer would use an appropriate arrowhead for his target. Armor-piercing "bodkin points" were sharp and narrow, while other heads were broader. Arrows often had barbs to make them harder to extract. The elaborate decoration on these arrows show that they belonged to someone of high rank.

**LONGBOWMEN**
In the 14th and 15th centuries, archers, trained from youth to use the longbow, were the prime instrument of English victory over the French in battles in the Hundred Years War (1337–1453) like Crécy, Poitiers, and Agincourt. This was mainly because French knights, used to hand-to-hand combat, were killed by the longbowmen as they charged toward successive hails of arrows.

**JAPANESE ARCHER**
Japanese war bows were made of bamboo and other wood combined and were longer than European longbows. Whereas a European knight would have considered it beneath his dignity to use a bow in battle, many samurai were skilled archers. They were trained from childhood to follow a strict code called the "warrior's way," and were prepared to fight to death for their overlord.

## CROSSBOW

The crossbow was popular in medieval Europe, and versions were used in China and Japan. In some lighter models the string was drawn back by means of a hook called a goat's-foot lever. Usually the bow was so powerful that its user needed a small winch, called a moulinet, to draw it. When the bow was drawn the moulinet was removed and the bolt was loaded. The crossbow was powerful and accurate, but it was slow to load and hard to protect from rain or damp. At Crécy (1346) the Genoese crossbowmen on the French side were outshot by English longbowmen.

## BOOMERANG

The boomerang is a curved throwing stick used for fighting or hunting by the Aboriginal Australians. Although some boomerangs were specially designed to return to the thrower, many were not. Similar weapons were used in Africa and India.

*Bowstring*

*Crossbow bolt with broad head used for battles and hunting*

*Groove for bolt*

*Crossbow bolt with steel armor-piercing tip*

*Hook hooked over bowstring, so that it could be drawn back*

*Hand grenade*

## NORTH BRITISH GRENADIER

The hand grenade was used in the 17th and 18th centuries when fortifications were attacked. Grenadiers wore a cap which made it easy for them to sling their musket over their shoulders, leaving both hands free. They used a length of smouldering cord (the match) to light the fuse on the grenade, an iron sphere filled with powder, before throwing it.

## CROSSBOWMEN

These crossbowmen are in action during the successful siege of Jerusalem by the Crusaders in 1099. While his companions shot, the soldier on the right is reloading his bow, putting one foot through the stirrup to hold it down and using the moulinet to wind back the string. Crossbowmen and archers sometimes worked in pairs, with one reloading behind a shield while the other fired.

*Windlass handle*

*Base of crossbow fitted into windlass*

# Maces and battle-axes

WIDELY USED BY KNIGHTS and warriors from the 11th to the 16th centuries, maces and battle-axes could be used to smash their way through helmets and body armor as well as chain mail. While armor offered good protection against edged weapons like swords or spears, some daggers were specially designed to defeat armor by penetrating where plates joined. It could be difficult to kill a dismounted knight if the right weapon was not at hand: at the battle of Bouvines, fought in 1214 near Lille in northern France, the French king, Philip Augustus, was surrounded by enemy footsoldiers, but they failed to kill him before help arrived.

*Armor-piercing spike*

*Flange*

*Long handle gave the user extra "swing"*

**SPIKED MACE**
Helmets were often designed to encourage blows to glance off them. This 18th-century Indian mace is embellished with spikes which would prevent it from slipping when it struck. Cruder spiked weapons—called "morning stars" or "holy water sprinklers"—were used in Europe.

*Grip*

*Top of handle protects hand*

*Weighted head helped the user to strike harder*

*Hammer head*

*Spike for penetrating armor*

**WAR HAMMER**
The war hammer was a popular weapon in Europe. It usually had a sharp point at the back, and a blunt head or a set of claws that would not slip on armor, at the front. This specimen is Polish or Hungarian and dates from about 1700.

*Ornamental studs*

**FLANGED MACE**
This mace, made in Italy in about 1550, has the weight to smash armor, and flanges that help it to penetrate the armor. Maces were often hung from a knight's saddle when not in use. They were sometimes carried by fighting clerics (churchmen) who were forbidden to shed blood!

**WARRIOR MONK**
Most Japanese warriors carried a two-handed Japanese sword that had a sharp, heavy blade. However, this redoubtable warrior monk is armed with a mighty club. These monks wore a mixture of military and monkish dress, with a cap instead of a helmet.

## PUNCHING DAGGER

The Indian fist-dagger was held by the grip, which runs at right angles to the blade, so that the blow was delivered by punching. This late-18th-century version has a double blade, but single blades with reinforced points for the penetration of armor were more common.

*Wrist guard*

*Grip*

*Serrated blades caused more damage to armor and opponent*

*Armor-piercing points*

**ROBERT THE BRUCE**
At Bannockburn (Scotland, 1314), an English knight, Sir Henry de Bohun, charged the Scottish king Robert the Bruce. Bruce deftly sidestepped and brained de Bohun, later remarking: "I have broke my good battle-ax."

*Ax head*

## PARRYING SHIELD

This rare weapon was used as a cross between a left-hand dagger and a shield. It was held in the left hand to parry a sword blow. It also enabled its user to stab an opponent's arm or body. Other types had a small shield mounted with two black buck horns.

*Blade*

*Shield with handgrip behind*

*Ornamental tassels*

## BATTLE-AX

This ornate battle-ax, from the Deccan region in central India, has a guard like that found on many Indian swords. The hilt unscrews to reveal a short sword blade. Indian weapons often displayed features like this that were ingenious but of doubtful value in battle. The Maratha Confederacy recruited many of its formidable soldiers from the Deccan; it was defeated by the British, led by the future Duke of Wellington, in 1803.

*Sword handle unscrews to reveal sword*

*Guard*

# Swords

The sword was used in prehistoric times and was still carried by cavalrymen as late as the end of World War I (1914–1918). There were two main types of sword. Cutting swords, such as medieval knights' cross-hilted swords or Highland officers' broadswords, had heavy blades with sharp edges. Stabbing swords, like the rapier, were lighter and had sharp points. Many military swords were general purpose "cut and thrust" weapons. Real damage in battle was usually done by well-directed thrusts that produced lethal wounds, rather than by cuts that were often deflected by an opponent's helmet.

*Hand and wrist fit inside steel gauntlet, which is held by a grip inside*

### SWORD DRILL
To use his sword effectively a soldier had to know how to attack his enemy, and to protect himself by parries (defensive strokes). This series of illustrations comes from an early-19th-century British drill book and shows exercises for the broadsword.

### LADIES FIGHTING
This 15th-century lady is wielding a knightly broadsword. Although women rarely took up arms in medieval Europe, in Japan women of samurai families were sometimes trained to use a light halberd (p. 45).

### SWORD-BREAKER
When men fought on foot with rapiers, they often carried a dagger in the left hand. A sword-breaker was also carried in the left hand, and its serrated edge was intended to catch an opponent's blade, which could then be broken with a twist of the wrist. It could also be used as a conventional dagger. This example was made in Italy in about 1660.

### GAUNTLET SWORD
A fighter's sword hand and forearm were in danger from an opponent's cuts. This 17th-century Indian gauntlet sword embodied protection for the hand and the wrist. Its blade was made in Solingen, a center of sword-production in Germany. Good-quality European blades were often used in Asia, and vice versa: attractively patterned "Damascus" blades are sometimes found on 19th-century European swords.

*Solingen maker's mark*

*Barbs to trap opponent's blade*

*Sharp edge*

*Broad, double-edged blade*

## CAVALRY CHARGE

Heavy cavalry usually carried straight, heavy swords and were trained to use them primarily for thrusting, leaning forward in the saddle with the sword arm outstretched. This illustration shows a famous German cavalry charge, known as "Von Bredow's Death-Ride," that took place in 1870 in the Franco-Prussian War. In practice, at that time, the infantry soldier who kept his head and used his rifle and bayonet to defend himself had a good chance of beating a cavalryman.

*Guard*

*Grip*

*Pommel*

## PAPPENHEIMER RAPIER

This rapier was named after the Graf zu Pappenheim, a general in the Thirty Years War (1618–1648, between the Catholic and Protestant forces in most of Europe). The complex hilt, with a combination of shell-shaped guards covering the hand and bars protecting the knuckles, was characteristic of this type of sword.

## BROADSWORD

This basket-hilted broadsword was carried by Scottish Highland officers at the time when infantry still used swords in battle. It is sometimes called a claymore, although that name initially referred to an earlier broadsword with a cross-shaped guard.

*A groove called a fuller added strength to blade; it was also less correctly known as a blood gutter*

HENRY
WILKINSON
PALL MALL
LONDON

*Maker's mark*

*Buckskin covered with red cloth*

*Pierced steel guard offers good protect*

# Firearms

**MUSKETEER**
This Scottish musketeer carries a matchlock musket, ignited by a smouldering cord (the match).

*Socket bayonet fitted into muzzle*

*Powder charges hang from bandolier*

IN THE 18TH AND 19TH centuries, most infantry soldiers carried a musket. This had a smooth-bore barrel and was loaded by inserting powder and shot into the muzzle and ramming it home. It had a short range and its black powder produced acrid smoke. A few specialists were equipped with rifles, whose barrels, cut with spiral grooves, spun the bullet to improve its range and accuracy. Inventors had long experimented with breechloading (rear-loading) weapons, but it was not until the middle of the 19th century that these became available on a large scale. Bayonets could be attached to the weapon's muzzle for close-quarter fighting.

**INFANTRY BATTLE**
French and Prussian infantry in a bayonet fight at Hegelbord, 1813. Close-quarter combat like this was actually much rarer than many artists suggested, as the shock effect of approaching bayonets often persuaded enemy soldiers to run.

*Cock holds flint*

*Frizzen struck by flint to produce spark*

*Barrel*

*Sling*

*Butt*

**THREE MUSKETEERS**
On the left, a 17th-century French musketeer bites the end of his cartridge off before tipping the contents into his musket; in the center a soldier rams home powder and shot, with the cartridge paper inserted last as wadding; on the right a soldier "gives fire."

*Lead shot*

*Patch box contains cloth patches, which were rammed down the barrel to ensure snug fit of the bullet*

**BULLET MOLD**
Instrument
...osed and
...h molten
...nake a
...all.

*Paper cartridge contained bullet and gunpowder*

*Lead musket balls*

## COLT .45
The US Colt Single-Action Army revolver was often known as the Peacemaker or the Frontier. The six chambers in the the cylinder were loaded singly with .45-in (1-cm) bullets, and the weapon was fired by pulling back the hammer and pressing the trigger. Empty cases were pushed out with the ejector.

*Hammer*

*Cylinder rotates with each shot*

*Ejector tube*

French 1866 Chassepot rifle, an early and very effective breechloader

*Loading gate*

*Trigger*

### LAST STAND
Men of the British 66th regiment at Maiwand near Kandahar in Afghanistan, in 1880, in the Second Afghan War (1878–1880). They are armed with the breechloading Martini-Henry rifle. Exaggerated confidence in its performance played a part in the defeat of the British at this battle.

*Flintlock*

*Barrel*

*Trigger*

*Ramrod*

### FRENCH PISTOL
French flintlock pistol, made in the government arsenal at St. Etienne. Weapons like this were usually carried in holsters at the front of the cavalryman's saddle.

*Butt*

*Bullet*

*Ramrod*

*Bayonet*

*Socket fit over muzzle of musket*

### MUSKET
A British Brown Bess musket, typical of the weapon carried by infantry in the Napoleonic Wars (1803–1815), had an effective range of about 300 ft (90 m). It was equipped with a socket bayonet, which slipped over the weapon's muzzle, allowing the soldier to load and fire with his bayonet fixed. This was an improvement on the earlier socket bayonet, which blocked the barrel of the gun.

*Blade of bayonet*

### RIFLE
The Baker rifle, named after its maker, the London gunsmith Ezekiel Baker, was carried by British rifle regiments in the Napoleonic period. Far more accurate than a musket, the Baker was effective at 900 ft (275 m).

*Sword bayonet, called a sword, that clipped on to the end of the Baker rifle*

# Close combat

**STORM FROM THE EAST**
Successive waves of invaders from Asia threatened Europe. These Mongol horsemen (p. 14), entirely at home in the saddle, were formidable opponents.

ANCIENT BATTLES were contests between warriors on foot or horseback. They struck out in close combat with bronze or iron weapons and used short-range missiles like arrows or javelins. Although battle tactics were usually simple, some commanders showed special skill, for example, by keeping a reserve of fresh troops on hand and using them when the enemy was exhausted. More often training or equipment gave the decisive advantage: the Roman army and the Greeks of Alexander the Great (356–323 BCE) were well armed and well organized and used carefully thought-out tactics. For thousands of years the infantry were superior, but with the invention of the stirrup the cavalry reigned almost unchecked until the development of firearms.

*Repair indicates that it was worn through many battles*

*Crest helped to deflect blows from enemy's sword*

**SAMURAI ARMOR**
Samurai showed their status as a warrior class by wearing a pair of swords and elaborate armor made of plates of lacquered metal linked with colored silk cord. This gave them some protection from sword cuts in close combat.

**WARRIOR QUEEN**
Not all women stayed at home while their menfolk were hunters and warriors. In the first century CE, Boudicca, the queen of a tribe living in East Anglia (England), fought against the occupying Romans. Although she destroyed three of the Romans' most important towns (London, St. Albans, and Colchester), she was eventually defeated by the Romans' superior tactics.

**PRE-ETRUSCAN HELMET**
Armor protected a soldier's most vulnerable points, and, therefore, added greatly to his chances of survival, but at the same time the weight slowed him down. This bronze helmet comes from Vulci in Italy and was made between 800 and 700 BCE. Although at this time iron had been introduced in Europe, bronze was still used for armor and weapons alike.

"Recover your halberd"

"Advance your halberd"

"Shoulder your halberd"

## HALBERD DRILL
Weapons with a blade or a spike on a long wooden handle are called pole arms or staff weapons. A weapon of this type, the halberd, survived from medieval times to become the characteristic weapon of European infantry sergeants throughout the 18th century. These figures demonstrate halberd drill.

## POLISH MACE
In the 17th century, Poland fielded impressive heavy cavalry who used lances, as well as maces like this early 17th-century specimen. The Polish king John Sobieski (1624–1696) led the army that beat the Turks besieging Vienna in 1683, a victory that helped keep most of Europe out of Turkish control.

*Sharp edge*

Swiss halberd, from around 1400

German poleax, early 16th century

*Maker's mark*

## REACHING OUT
Poleaxes and halberds increased the infantry soldiers' reach and were very useful if they were dealing with horsemen. The Swiss gained an awesome reputation by using pikemen who carried long spears, assisted by halberdiers. Charles the Bold, Duke of Burgundy (1433–1477), was killed in battle against the Swiss at Nancy, his head split open by a halberd blow.

*Langets (metal strips) protect staff*

Mounted knights carry steel-tipped lances and a pennant

## KNIGHT IN ARMOR
Armored knights, charging with lances on their heavy horses, were the dominant force in medieval Europe. There were some foes, like Swiss pikemen or English archers, whom they found hard to deal with. Monarchs liked to be depicted as knights even when these warriors were losing their value: this illustration shows the Emperor Charles V of Spain in 1529.

# Gunpowder arms

THE INVENTION OF GUNPOWDER, a mixture of explosive chemicals, led to the invention of firearms. In these weapons a controlled explosion of gunpowder in one part of the firearm sent a bullet or a cannonball down a barrel. In fact, gunpowder did not change war at a stroke: in the 16th and 17th centuries a mixture of old and new techniques were used in battles, with swords and pikes alongside muskets and cannons. For most of that period infantry and cavalry alike used firearms and edged weapons. Infantry consisted of pikemen, with body armor and long spears, and musketeers armed with muskets. Cavalrymen carried swords and pistols, but the steady increase of infantry firepower limited their effectiveness. Most armies drew up with their infantry in the center and the cavalry on the flanks. Cannons, still relatively cumbersome and primitive, were placed in the gaps between blocks of infantry.

**FIRING A VOLLEY**
"Volley guns" or "ribaldequins" had numerous barrels that were fired more or less simultaneously. In this specimen, shown in a French publication of 1630, the gunner fires the barrels one at a time.

**OLIVER CROMWELL**
Cromwell (1599–1658) was an English country gentleman and Member of Parliament who helped raise the Parliamentarian army on the outbreak of the English Civil War in 1642. He became lieutenant-general (second-in-command) of the New Model Army and played a leading role in winning the decisive battle of Naseby (1645).

*Cock (with flint) lowered onto revolving wheel*

**PISTOLS**
Muskets, with their longer barrels, were difficult to use on horseback. The first pistols, which were handheld weapons, were wheel-lock pistols. The wheel was wound up with a key, and when the trigger was pressed it revolved, striking sparks from a flint held in the cock.

*Revolving wheel with toothed edge*

*Trigger*

*Ring for carrying cord*

Rammer, to force charge and bullet down gun barrel

*Nozzle*

Wrench to wind up wheel on pistol

**POWDER FLASK**
The nozzle of this powder flask has two spring-loaded catches. The one nearer to the flask was opened to let powder flow into the nozzle. It was then closed, trapping a measured quantity of powder, which was loaded into the weapon by opening the upper catch.

**GUSTAVUS ADOLPHUS**
The Thirty Years War (1618–1648), in which Protestants fought Catholics, was the most destructive conflict of the period in Europe. The Swedish king Gustavus Adolphus (1594–1632) was a champion of the Protestant cause. He produced a reliable professional army that he commanded with skill and courage, only to be killed at Lützen, halfway through the conflict.

**HEAD WEAR**

**Comb**
*protected
head from
sword blows*

**Peak protected**
*top half of face*

The burgonet, so called because it originated in Burgundy, was widely worn by cavalrymen and infantry officers in the 16th century. This specimen, produced in Germany in about 1590, is made of blackened steel, held together by rivets decorated with gilt stars. Armor was often blued or blackened by a chemical process to make it much less likely to rust on campaign.

*Hinged cheekpieces*

*Lower part
of burgonet
protected neck*

*End fits
into muzzle
of musket*

*Scabbard*

*Catch to
release blades*

*Blades come
together to
create a
single dagger*

**PLUG BAYONET**
The first bayonets were jammed into the musket's muzzle, which meant that the weapon could not be fired while the bayonet was fixed. This unusual and elaborate French bayonet of about 1660 had a stud near the hilt that released two spring-loaded portions of the blade. This was more to disconcert the enemy than to create greater damage.

**BREASTPLATE**

*Stud for
shoulder strap*

Breastplates and backplates were often worn with helmets after other armor had disappeared. A breastplate like this would defeat sword cuts and keep out pistol and musket balls. Its edges were turned out at the neck, shoulders, and waist to encourage a sword or lance-point to slip off. Two straps attached to the backplate passed over the shoulders to fasten to the studs on the breastplate.

*Turned-out edges
also make the
breastplate and
the backplate
more comfortable*

*Raised part
of breastplate
encourages
sword cuts
to glance off*

**CAVALRY SWORD**
This sword, with its robust double-edged blade that could be used for both cutting and thrusting, has a steel "swept-hilt" handguard. It was made in Munich, in southern Germany, in about 1600, and it is typical of the cavalry weapons of the period.

*Handguard*

*Continued on next page*

*Cartridge top held safely in place by button*

# Large armies

In the early 18th century, battles took on a form they were to retain for many years. The majority of combatants were footsoldiers (infantry) armed with flintlock muskets, and battles centered on ferocious close-range exchanges of fire between the opposing infantrymen. Light cavalry scouted, screened (carried out counterreconnaissance activities), and pursued, and heavy cavalry charged hostile horsemen and rode down shaken infantry. Cannonballs, multiple shot, and shells caused dreadful casualties in the enemy's closely packed ranks. For most of the 18th century, armies were composed of both volunteers and men pressed into service. Frederick the Great (1712–1786) tried to recruit foreigners so as not to ruin Prussian industry and agriculture: in 1768 he had 70,000 native soldiers in an army of 160,000. The French Revolution changed all this. In 1793 the Revolutionary government, threatened by invasion, declared that all able-bodied men were to serve, and the army may have reached a million men in mid-1794, ushering in the age of mass armies.

**AMMUNITION POUCH**
This white metal pouch was made in the Caucasus in the late 18th century and would have contained paper cartridges for a musket or a pistol. There is a clip at the back for attaching it to the belt.

**CARTRIDGE CASE**
This cartridge case is one of a pair that buttoned onto its owner's coat. In the heat of action, it was important to have easy access to ammunition. Russian Cossacks wore these as late as World War II.

**PISTOLS**
Many cavalrymen carried a pair of pistols in holsters at the front of their saddles. These were made in the Caucasus, an area subject to Russian and Turkish influence, and are decorated with embossed silverwork that appears to have an Asian influence.

**LIGHT DRAGOON**
This private of the British 13th Light Dragoons is practicing parrying, or deflecting, a cut aimed at his horse's head by an enemy horseman. His curved saber is typical of that carried by light cavalry, who used their swords for cutting rather than thrusting. His carbine (a short musket) would normally have been clipped to the carbine belt passing over his left shoulder. The 13th served with the Duke of Wellington in Spain in the Peninsular War (1808–1814).

**NAPOLEON**
Napoleon Bonaparte (1769–1821) was an artillery officer who became emperor of the French in 1804. He dominated Europe, winning a series of victories, but exhausted his army when they retreated from Moscow in Russia's inhospitable winter (1812) and was then defeated at Waterloo (1815). He was brilliantly successful in using corps (large groups of regiments of all arms) that moved on separate routes but fought united.

**DETTINGEN**
In 1743 an Allied army under George II beat the French at Dettingen on the Main River. It was the last time a king of England commanded in battle. Contemporary illustrations fail to show just how smoky battlefields were. A veteran of an earlier battle saw no light "but what the fire of the volleys of shot gave."

*6-lb (2.7-kg) cannonball*

**CANNONBALLS**
Solid shot was the most common artillery projectile. Gunners usually tried to obtain a ricochet effect: they fired cannonballs that hit the ground just in front of their target and then bounced through it, causing casualties with every bound. This technique required firm ground, and the effect of Napoleon's main battery of guns at Waterloo was spoiled by soggy terrain.

*Bronze gun barrel*

*Replacement gun carriage*

**BURMESE DRAGON**
Superior military technology sometimes gave European armies a decisive advantage when they were fighting overseas, although determined local people who knew the ground proved to be serious adversaries. Asian and African rulers sometimes hired European military experts and bought modern weapons. This cannon was made in Portugal for the king of Burma (now Myanmar). It is a decorative piece but would have worked had the need arisen. The barrel was captured by the British in 1885 and is mounted on a replacement carriage.

# Rifled weapons

FROM THE MID-19TH CENTURY onward, technology changed the face of battle. Weapons gained accuracy by becoming rifled (with a grooved barrel), and rate of fire by becoming breechloading (back-loading). Black powder was replaced by smokeless powder, and new high explosives increased the effect of shells. Machine guns developed into mobile weapons that provided "the concentrated essence of infantry." It took armies some time to assimilate the effects of new technology, but the firepower revolution eventually produced battlefields that seemed strangely empty: by World War I (1914–1918) whole armies took refuge in trenches. A British artillery officer wrote that "there were thousands of hidden men in front of me … but nobody moved, everybody was waiting for the safety of darkness."

*Magazine gave out ammunition as it was needed*

*Foresight aligned with the backsight to aim gun*

*Backsight*

*Crank to fire gun*

*Gear to elevate (raise) and depress (lower) barrel*

**BREECHLOADERS INTO BATTLE**
The Franco-Prussian War of 1870–1871 was the first war in which infantrymen on both sides carried breechloaders. Heavy losses were suffered in charges against determined infantry, and by the end of the war the Germans reduced casualties by attacking with "fire and maneuver" in which some soldiers fired while others rushed forward to fire in turn.

**POM-POM AMMUNITION**
By 1900 fast-firing light cannons were in service in several armies. Christened pom-poms because of their sound, they were subsequently used as antiaircraft weapons.

*Tripod*

**GARDNER GUN**
In 1874 William Gardner, who had served in the Civil War (1861–1865), invented a machine gun that was much lighter than most contemporary weapons. Most of its versions had two barrels to create a high rate of fire, and some had five. The Gardner gun was adopted by the British Royal Navy, and unlike many early machine guns, it was actually used in battle, at El Teb and Tamai in the Sudan in 1884.

## LEE-ENFIELD RIFLE
In 1902 the British army adopted the .303-in Lee-Enfield short magazine rifle as the best and latest technology. A trained soldier could fire at least 15 rounds a minute with it, and it had an effective range of up to 3,600 ft (1,097 m).

Sword bayonet

## INDIAN WARS
In the 1870s, US cavalrymen used single-shot Springfield carbines, but discovered that some of their opponents had traded hides for much-superior Winchester repeaters.

US cavalrymen in action during the Indian Wars of the 1870s

## BOER BANDOLIER
Ammunition consisting of smokeless powder in metallic cases was easy to carry and store.

## RIFLED BARREL
Rifling describes the grooves in a weapon's barrel which spin the bullet to make it go farther faster. There were many systems. This is the Whitworth hexagonal system, used in some British-made cannons imported by the Confederates during the Civil War.

*Twisted grooves*

## BATTLE OF FORT WAGNER
Slavery helped cause the US Civil War, as slavery was banned in the North but important for working on plantations in the South. The Union army (of the North) used black soldiers in segregated regiments with white officers. 5,000 Union soldiers, including the 54th Massachusetts (Colored) Volunteers, attacked Fort Wagner on Charleston harbour on 18 July 1863. They reached the fort but could not take it, and lost 1,500 men.

## ROBERT E. LEE
Lee (1807–1870) commanded the main Confederate army during the Civil War. He defended Northern Virginia, preventing superior Union armies from taking the Confederate capital of Richmond, and invaded the North twice.

# Communications

The heliograph, a tripod-mounted mirror, used sunlight to create flashes. Long and short flashes made up letters of the alphabet. It worked well in areas like the northwest frontier of India, which were often sunny and had long views.

*Sight*

*A heliograph's mirror could be adjusted to send messages in any direction*

*Tripod*

THE US GENERAL Omar Bradley (1893–1981) wrote that "Congress makes a man a general: communications make him a commander." On the battlefield itself, soldiers needed to communicate, although their ability to do so was impeded by noise, smoke, and confusion. Senior commanders had to know what was happening in battle in order to commit fresh troops or change their line of attack. Often inadequate communications, not lack of skill or courage, ruined a promising plan. Until the development of the telegraph in the mid-19th century, communications changed little. Staff officers or messengers delivered verbal or written messages. Regimental officers used their own voices or relayed orders through drummers and trumpeters. Messages could be sent over longer distances by signaling systems or heliographs.

**PIGEONS FOR RECONNAISSANCE**
French cavalry in 1897 sending messages by carrier pigeons. Their main limitation was that they simply flew back to their lofts, so messages could only be sent one way.

**MESSAGE CARRIERS**
Pigeons with messages attached to their legs in carriers like these were widely used during World War I, when the largely static nature of trench warfare reduced their limitations. The last message sent from Fort Vaux at Verdun, fiercely attacked by the Germans in 1916, asked for help and warned: "This is my last pigeon."

*Cord for hanging trumpet across shoulder later became purely decorative*

*Decorative tassels*

**TRUMPET**
Cavalry used the trumpet to transmit orders down the chain of command. In the British army troopers memorized calls by putting words to them. The call for "pursue" had the words: "Tis the 'Pursue,' make 'em run!"

**TRUMPETER**
This 19th-century trumpeter of the British Household Cavalry had an elaborate banner attached to his trumpet. Banners were mostly reserved for ceremonial occasions.

**DRUMMER**
Drummers usually wore a uniform of their regiment's facing color (the color of the main uniform's collar and cuffs) with distinctive lace embellishments. This drummer belonged to the British 15th Light Dragoons in 1768.

**SMOKE SIGNALS**
The need for communication was not confined to formally organized armies. American Indians were skilled at communicating by smoke signals, using a blanket to release smoke in puffs whose meaning could be understood by distant observers. One of the causes of Major General Custer's defeat by Sitting Bull at the Battle of Little Big Horn (1876) was poor contact between advancing columns of cavalry.

**WHISTLE**
Whistle blasts could be distinguished, in the din of battle, when shouts might not. Officers in rifle and light infantry regiments, whose men frequently were spread out, used whistles more often than their comrades in line regiments. The crossbelt, with an ammunition pouch at the back and a whistle suspended by a chain on the front, was widely worn by officers of rifle regiments and has been retained for full dress by the British Royal Green Jackets (p. 12).

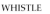

*Drum skin*

*Chain kept whistle from being lost*

*Slider kept drum skin taught*

**CIVIL WAR DRUM**
Soldiers memorized tunes that regulated life in camp and transmitted orders on the battlefield. If an army was to form up ready to fight, its soldiers would be woken that morning by the long roll of the general call to arms, rather than by the usual reveille (the wake-up call). The drum was used by the infantry, although the bugle, with its better carrying power, became increasingly popular.

*Wood shell*

*US national symbol*

*The whistle was stored in this socket attached to the cross-belt when it was not in use*

# Engineering

MILITARY ENGINEERS helped an army to fight, move, and live. Engineers were particularly concerned with building permanent fortifications and with besieging fortresses. The French engineer Vauban (1633–1707) was responsible for a deep belt of fortifications protecting the borders of France. For many years engineer and artillery officers were better trained than infantry or cavalry officers, to reflect the need to master a range of technical skills. Engineers also constructed field fortifications (including trenches), built or destroyed bridges, made roads and, latterly, railroads, and improved the comfort and sanitation of barracks and camps. Some even established reputations as architects.

**MEDIEVAL SIEGE**
For centuries fortifications and siegecraft were the engineer's chief tasks. The walls of medieval castles were high and thick, making it difficult to get over or through them. Engineers often dug beneath them, making huge underground chambers with roofs held up by wooden props. These chambers, called mines, were packed with inflammable material. When it burned the props collapsed, and with them the walls of the castle.

**TRENCH LOOKOUT**
In September 1914 the firepower of modern weapons helped freeze the war of mobility into the stalemate of trench warfare. Elaborate trench systems, with several mutually supporting lines, ran across Belgium and northern France.

*Slope to absorb gun's recoil*

*Eyepiece*

**PERISCOPE**
Trench warfare encouraged all kinds of ingenuity to enable soldiers to survive in what comfort could be found in trenches and dugouts. Because snipers (specially trained riflemen) were ready to shoot men who looked over the top of a trench, periscopes were produced that enabled them to observe in safety.

**BUILDING BRIDGES**
Engineers built bridges as well as destroying them. Some bridges rested on floating pontoons; others were suspended on ropes and poles.

**TRAINING**
Fortification was a science with rules that engineers had to master. These 19th-century British Royal Engineers trained by building a scale model of fortifications. The broad, low earth walls are designed to resist artillery fire.

*Pedal to release cannon*

### EDELSBERG BRIDGE

A retreating army could buy time by destroying bridges, forcing the enemy to build their own. It was a matter of fine judgment as to when bridges should be demolished. Here we see the French attacking Austrians on a bridge near Vienna in 1809, while Austrian engineers try to hack it down to keep the French on the other side.

### FRENCH SAPPER

Digging zigzag trenches toward a besieged fortress was called "sapping," so engineers were often known as sappers. In most armies, infantry regiments contained specialists in field engineering. They were not as widely trained as proper engineers. These men carried axes and wore thick aprons to protect their uniforms. They often sported distinctive beards.

*Brass gun barrel*

*The cannon would fire over a parapet (bank of tightly packed earth) or through an embrasure (gap in the fortifications)*

### FORTRESS GUN

Cannons used in fortresses had garrison carriages with smaller wheels than field artillery. This gun sat on a special platform. When it was fired, the gun's recoil sent it up the slope until it passed over a stop that prevented it from rolling forward. It could then be reloaded by its crew, who had only to press the pedal to let the gun roll forward ready for firing.

### STRASBOURG

Sieges were often contests between the defensive technology of the engineer and the offensive technology of the gunner. It was easier for the latter to develop new weapons than it was for engineers to prepare effective defenses, and fortresses easily became outdated. In 1870 the Germans blew a gap in the defenses of Strasbourg and set fire to parts of the town, forcing the governor to surrender.

*Wheels enable cannons to be moved sideways to point cannons in different directions*

# Victory and defeat

ALTHOUGH SOME BATTLES were drawn, with no winner or loser, in most, one side defeated the other. Victory was indicated by the killing or capturing of large numbers of opponents, driving the enemy from the battlefield, or seizing a town or a geographical feature. Sometimes the effects of victory were far-reaching. The Battle of Waterloo (1815) ended the reign of Napoleon and led to a period of stability in Europe. But there was no guarantee that battle would be decisive, and sometimes a long war exhausted both sides. The victor's gains might not justify the human cost of battle. After Waterloo, the British commander, the Duke of Wellington, remarked: "I don't know what it is to lose a battle, but certainly nothing can be more painful than to gain one with the loss of so many of one's friends."

**CORONATION OF NAPOLEON**
In classical times the laurel symbolized victory, and successful Roman generals who were granted a "triumph" were crowned with laurel and rode through Rome in a chariot. Napoleon wore a crown of laurel at his coronation in 1804 to show that he was a victorious military leader.

Big Elk, a warrior of the Omaha tribe

**VICTORIOUS WARRIOR**
Many Plains Native Americans changed their appearance in some way to show their victories. Big Elk, a warrior of the Omaha tribe, blackened his face to show that he had recently killed an enemy. Victory was also demonstrated by taunting an enemy with a nonlethal blow.

**INSTRUMENTS OF VICTORY**
Past victories can help win future ones. Soldiers were encouraged to take pride in their regiment's achievements, commemorated in battle honors emblazoned on its colors. These British guardsmen fought fiercely at the Battle of Inkerman (Crimea, 1854) although heavily outnumbered by attacking Russians. Their victory brought a new battle honor.

**LOOTING AND PILLAGING**
There was often a profit motive in war. Many European noblemen who went on the First Crusade in 1095 were landless younger sons hoping for land in the Middle East. Captured knights were held for ransom and were released only when their families had paid the money. Common soldiers would pillage if allowed to: here we see a 14th-century army leaving a town it has just sacked, with livestock and other loot. Civilians were the real losers in most campaigns. They were robbed and maltreated by armies that passed by and a long conflict might leave little more than a desert behind it.

### PRISONERS AT THE FRONT
Prisoners were sometimes well looked after by the soldiers who captured them but found that treatment worsened in prisoner-of-war camps. These Confederates were captured by Union forces in the Civil War (1861–1865).

### MARQUETRY BOX
A series of international agreements have attempted to ensure that soldiers who surrendered in or after battle were well treated by their captors. Life as a prisoner of war was at best extremely boring, and prisoners often whiled away the hours, and made a little money, by manufacturing trinkets. This straw marquetry box was made by a Napoleonic French prisoner of war in Edinburgh Castle and sold to a local merchant in exchange for provisions.

### GIVING UP ARMS
This sword was surrendered by the French governor of Ciudad Rodrigo, in Spain, to Lieutenant John Gurwood, who led the attack on this fortress in 1812 during the Peninsular War (1808–1814). Officers gave up their swords as a sign of surrender.

*Inscription recording the history of the sword*

*Classical figure of victory*

*Snake's head popped up when lid was opened*

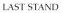

### BOOTS
These toy boots were made by a Boer captured by the British during the Boer War (South Africa) of 1899–1902 and sent to a camp in the West Indies. In addition to taking prisoners of war, the British removed Boer women and children from outlying farms to prevent them from helping Boer columns, and housed them in camps where many of them died from disease.

### LAST STAND
The last stand of a determined group of soldiers who fight to the death rather than surrender is a popular image for military artists. Here we see a group of British soldiers surrounded by the Boers of Modderfontein in 1901. Such occurrences were relatively rare unless members of the losing side knew that they would be killed if they were taken prisoner.

*Inscription shows that sword was made in the Spanish city of Toledo, famous for its high-quality metalwork*

# Rewards of battle

**REGIMENTAL ORDER**
In Britain, medals were not generally issued until the 19th century, and this lack of official awards encouraged regiments to produce their own. This order of the 37th was instituted by Sir Eyre Coote of the 37th Regiment in 1774.

MEDALS, ORDERS, AND DECORATIONS are among the rewards of battle. Medals are given for gallantry, to commemorate an event, for service in a war, battle, or campaign, and for long service or good conduct. Orders of knighthood harken back to medieval knights and have several classes—like a club with members of varying status. They are awarded for a variety of achievements, although some orders are specifically military. Decorations, which are granted for distinguished deeds or bravery, are generally superior to medals but usually lack the different classes found in orders.

**DUKE OF WELLINGTON**
The Duke of Wellington (1769–1852) commanded the British army that fought the French in Spain and at Waterloo. Here he wears his Gold Cross (a British decoration) as well as the stars of several orders, including the Spanish Order of the Golden Fleece. The Duke, like many senior officers in coalition armies, received numerous foreign orders.

**ORDERS**
Many orders of knighthood have separate military and civilian divisions, although some are purely military. In full dress uniform, knights wear the star of their order, and the more senior classes of knight wear, in addition, a broad sash over the shoulder. In undress (less formal) uniform, membership of an order will be shown simply by a ribbon worn on the left breast.

**BRITAIN**
The Most Honorable Order of the Bath traces its origins to 1399. This breast star was worn with a red sash.

**THE NETHERLANDS**
The Military Order of William was founded by King William I of the Netherlands in 1815 and was awarded for bravery, leadership, and devotion to duty in the presence of the enemy.

**FRANCE**
The *Légion d'honneur* was established by Napoleon in 1802. It had several classes, for both military and civilian achievement.

**MEDALS FOR BRAVERY**
Some awards can only be given for bravery in the face of the enemy and are open to servicemen of all ranks. They are often less elaborate than the badges or stars of orders, but are highly prized. A recipient of the Victoria Cross, for example, puts the letters VC, which follow his name, before those for any other awards.

The Victoria Cross, the most coveted British decoration, was instituted in 1856

The New Zealand Cross was instituted by the New Zealand government in 1869

The Medal of Honor, established in 1861, is the US's highest award for bravery

The German Iron Cross was freely awarded for acts of bravery

The Prussian order *Pour le Mérite* became the highest award for gallantry in action

The British Waterloo Medal was awarded to all ranks who were present at the battle (1815)

The Queen's South Africa medal was awarded to British soldiers who fought in the Boer War (1899–1902)

The bars on this Military General Service Medal mark actions in Spain in 1812

The Egyptian bronze star awarded to British soldiers in the Egyptian campaigns of 1882–1885

## CAMPAIGN MEDALS

Campaign medals are awarded to individuals for participation in particular campaigns. The different battles the soldier had fought in might be named on bars attached to the ribbon; with some medals, for example, the Army Gold Medal, a new medal was awarded after a certain number of bars had been awarded. The recipient's name is usually engraved around the rim of British campaign medals.

The Army Gold Medal was given to senior British officers who fought in specific battles in 1806–1814

### TURKEY

The Turkish Order of Osmanieh was first instituted in 1861–1862 and was awarded to many British officers for their work in Egypt and the Sudan, which were then parts of the Turkish Empire.

### RUSSIA

The Order of Saint Anne was founded in Germany in 1735 and was taken over as an Imperial Russian order in 1797. This is an early version of the insignia.

### JAPAN

The star of the Japanese Order of the Rising Sun was established in 1875 and has eight classes.

### PORTUGAL

The Portuguese Military Order of St. Benedict of Aviz began as a religious military order but became secular (non-religious) in 1789. Its badge is a distinctive "cross fleury" (a cross with petal-shaped edges) enameled in green.

### BRITAIN

The Most Exalted Order of the Star of India was instituted by Queen Victoria in 1861.

# Sick and wounded

**A SURGEON AT WORK**
This 16th-century German surgeon is removing a crossbow bolt from a soldier's chest. The French surgeon Ambroise Paré, who lived at this time, was one of the fathers of military medicine. He disagreed with treating wounds with boiling oil and used a mixture of egg yolk, rose oil, and turpentine instead! With his English contemporaries, Paré did much to improve the status of military doctors.

WOUNDS AND DEATH are commonplace in war, but for hundreds of years many more soldiers died from disease than were killed by the enemy. Ignorance about the bacterial causes of disease long meant that many simple wounds proved fatal, because they were not properly cleaned and dirty instruments were used without being washed between operations. In the Civil War (1861–1865), for example, 96,000 Union men died in battle but almost twice as many died of disease. Discoveries in medicine and the organization of military medical services improved conditions, but it was not until the Boer War (1899–1902) that a soldier who had an amputation was more likely to survive than to die of gangrene.

**RED CROSS ARMBAND**
A Swiss banker named Henri Dunant was so shocked when he visited the battlefield of Solferino (Italy) in 1859 that he wrote a book about his experience. This led to the founding of the International Red Cross.

**FLORENCE NIGHTINGALE**
During the Crimean War (1853–1856) the British base hospital at Scutari in Turkey was in an appalling state, with the sick and wounded lying in corridors, and toilets and drains overflowing. By November 1854 almost half the patients had died. That month Florence Nightingale (1820–1910) arrived with 38 nurses. Their efforts helped to reduce the death rate to just 2.3 percent within six months. There were others who worked to help wounded soldiers, such as Mary Seacole, a Jamaican-born nurse who also ran a boarding house and store.

**NURSE'S INSTRUMENTS**
Nurses needed instruments to help them dress patients' wounds, cut bandages, and take temperatures. During the Crimean War nursing became an integral part of the armed forces.

**SURGEON'S SAW**
At Waterloo (1815) the Earl of Uxbridge was hit just below the knee by one of the last cannon-shots fired. This saw was used to amputate his wounded limb. The Earl survived the operation and was fitted with an artificial limb. This earned him the nickname "Old Peg-Leg."

*Florence Nightingale presented this set to a nurse in 1879*

*Instruments fit neatly into case*

HELEN BLOWER.
FROM
FLORENCE NIGHTINGALE
JANY 1ST 1879.
JOHN WEISS & SON. 82. STRAND. LONDON.

**THE BATTLE OF INKERMAN**
This Crimean battle in the fog cost the British and French over 4,000 casualties and the Russians 12,000. One officer wrote: "I have never witnessed in all my days such a frightful scene of human misery." This picture gives a rosy view of the medical facilities available.

**MEDICAL CHEST**
Doctors and some nurses equipped themselves with traveling chests containing a wide variety of medicines. This mid-19th-century chest contains stoppered bottles with liquid and powdered medicines that include sedatives and disinfectants. In the drawer there are pharmaceutical scales for weighing powders and the needle for a syringe.

*Bottles fit into slots so that they did not break in transit*

*Ipecacuanha, used to treat coughs and to induce vomiting*

*Quinine, used to treat fevers*

Quinine
1 to 10 grains.

HOLLOWAY DOWN
vident Dispens
LEYTONSTONE ROAD

POISON

Tonic Pills
HOLLOWAY DOWN
PROVIDENT DISPENSARY.

Cough Pills
HOLLOWAY DOWN
PROVIDENT DISPENSARY.

*Minim measure, to measure out medicine precisely*

*Disinfectant*

*Pills for soothing and curing coughs*

**COMMEMORATIVE MEDAL**
This British medal marks the 200th anniversary of the capture of Quebec by Major General James Wolfe in 1759.

# Memories of war

WAR IS REMEMBERED in many ways. Some participants thrust dark memories deep into their minds and prefer not to discuss their experiences. It is perhaps true to say that "those that know don't tell, and those that tell don't know." Others recall their exploits with pride and look back to a time when they felt valued and had comrades upon whom they could rely. Societies often recognize the sacrifice that soldiers have made on their behalf and commemorate their achievements with war memorials. All too often, though, returning soldiers found themselves neglected; when Frederick the Great of Prussia (1712–1786) saw ex-soldiers begging, he would sometimes say "drive the scum away." Other monarchs did their best for veterans. Louis XIV of France (1638–1715) established the Invalides in Paris as a home for wounded soldiers.

*Valley of the "Shadow of death."*

**FLOWERS OF THE FIELD**
Even after casualties have been removed and nature has healed the scars, battlefields remain poignant places. Lady Hornby, the wife of the British commissioner to Turkey during the Crimean War (1853–1856), pressed flowers from its battlefields. The flower (left) was picked in the "Valley of the Shadow of Death," the scene of the Charge of the Light Brigade (1854), and the flower (below) grew at Inkerman, the scene of another Crimean War battle, which took place in 1854.

**CAMERAMEN IN DANGER**
Newspaper reports from battlefields provided an independent record of events and helped civilians to understand the experiences of combatants. Today, television reports bring up-to-date battle news.

*Inkermann*

### MAN OF STONE

Edward the Black Prince (1330–1376), eldest son of the British king Edward III, fought in the Hundred Years War (1337–1453) at Crécy and Poitiers, both in France. His nickname originated from his black armor. He was a successful soldier and was honored with a burial in Canterbury Cathedral beneath an effigy that shows him in full armor.

### WAR MEMORIAL

Britain and its empire lost a million men in World War I (1914–1918). Their memorials range from tablets in village churches to massive arches and obelisks. This one honors the British Foot Guards.

### BURIAL

Prompt and reverend disposal of the dead is crucial for the morale of survivors: no soldier likes to think of lying forgotten on the battlefield. Here we see Japanese dead being buried during the Russo-Japanese War of 1904–1905.

### AMERICAN CEMETERY

It was not until World War I that burial of the dead was systematically organized, and policies then adopted by the British and Americans were continued into World War II. The American National Cemetery and Memorial at St. Laurent in Normandy has 9,286 graves, including those of 34 pairs of brothers and one father and son.

### CRUCIFIX

This crucifix was found on a dead Russian in the Crimea. The image of the crucified Christ is a compelling one for many Christian soldiers, who link their own suffering with his. Soldiers frequently became very attached to religious symbols and goodluck charms and became deeply depressed if they were accidentally lost.

### ICON

The unpredictable nature of war often deepens a soldier's religious faith (though sometimes it does the opposite) or makes him superstitious. Russian soldiers often carried icons (religious pictures) around their necks.

# World War II

Between 1939 and 1945, 70 million people died in the worst conflict in history—World War II. It was a struggle between the Allies—Britain, Soviet Russia, and the United States (aided by Australia, Canada, France, New Zealand, and others)—against the Axis powers, an alliance of Germany, Italy, and Japan. At first, the Axis powers enjoyed great success, but the Allies eventually triumphed. The turning points were Russia repulsing German forces in Eastern Europe in 1942, the US victory over Japan at the Battle of Midway in the same year, and the Allied invasion of Normandy to liberate German-occupied France in 1944.

Air crew load bombs on to a British Hawker Typhoon fighter-bomber

## BATTLEFIELD AIR POWER

While heavy bombers laid waste to industry, lighter planes became important battlefield weapons. In the early years of the war, the Stuka dive-bomber played key role in Germany's successful *blitzkrieg* ("lightning war") tactics. But by the time of the Allied invasion of Normandy in 1944, the Allies largely controlled the skies. Their fighter-bombers wreaked havoc on German ground forces with bombs, cannons, machine guns, and rockets.

British paratroop badge, 1940–1960

Canadian paratroop badge, 1940–1960

Bombsight from a German Junkers Ju-88 aircraft

## STRATEGIC BOMBING

After World War I, military planners came to believe that future conflicts could be won by using air power to strike at an opponent's industry. This would destroy its ability to produce weapons and military supplies and break the morale of its people. In World War II, Allied heavy bombers devastated German and Japanese cities, causing terrible civilian casualties. Strategic bombing did not, as some people had predicted, win the war outright, but it made a significant contribution to the Allied victory.

## AIRBORNE ASSAULTS

Germany's invasion of the Mediterranean island of Crete in 1941 was led by parachute and glider troops. These airborne troops could land behind enemy lines to take the opposition by surprise. American and British airborne forces held the flanks in Normandy in 1944. Later that year, Operation Market Garden was a bold but unsuccessful attempt by Allied parachutists to secure bridges in German-occupied Holland.

## RUSIAN FRONT

When the Germans attacked Soviet Russia in 1941 they came close to winning, but the onset of winter left them tantalizingly short of victory. The Germans resumed their advance in 1942, but were brought to a halt at the Russian city of Stalingrad on the Volga River. The Russians gradually pushed the Germans out of Russia, and rolled them back across Eastern Europe to take Berlin, the German capital, in 1945. At the war's end, the Russians controlled most of Eastern Europe, greatly influencing the shape of the postwar world (*see* pp. 66–67).

German troops in Russia, 1941

## BATTLE OF THE ATLANTIC

The Allies' ability to keep sea routes open across the Atlantic was key to their success. Merchant ships brought vital supplies from North America to Britain and Soviet Russia, and also US troops to fight in Europe. German U-boat submarine "wolf packs" hunted down and torpedoed supply ships and their naval escorts. Improved Allied warships, better detection equipment, and aircraft support, aided by intelligence from decoded German radio messages, gradually gave the Allies the upper hand.

PROPELLED WEAPONS

TORPEDO

DEPTH CHARGES

Cigarette cards showing antisubmarine torpedoes and depth charges

Australian troops assault a desert stronghold

## WAR IN NORTH AFRICA

In 1939, the Italians held Libya, while Egypt was under British protection. An Italian invasion of Egypt was repelled by the British in the winter of 1940–1941, but Germany then sent its *Afrikakorps* force into the desert war. See-saw advances and retreats followed. The British 8th Army's victory at the Battle of El Alamein in October 1942 finally turned the tide of the North African conflict in the Allies' favour.

Prayer flag carried by a Japanese serviceman

## WAR IN THE PACIFIC

At the start of their war against the Allies, the Japanese rampaged across the Pacific region. But defeat to US forces at the naval battle of Midway in June 1942 saw the balance tilt against them. The Americans advanced in the face of fierce defense. The capture of the Marianas Islands brought US bombers within striking range of the Japanese mainland. Dropping atomic bombs on the cities of Hiroshima and Nagasaki in August 1945 finally broke Japanese resolve.

## TANK WARFARE

Developed by the British and French in WWI, the tank came into its own in World War II. In 1939–1941, the Germans used it to great effect in its *blitzkrieg* tactics, where it was deployed with infantry, self-propelled artillery, and close air support. The US-made M4 Sherman was the main tank used by the Allies, but it faced formidable opposition in the German Panther and Tiger tanks. By the war's end it was the Russians, with their tough, reliable T-34, who had the advantage in tank warfare. The T-34 remained the mainstay of Russia's armored divisions in the postwar years.

US-made Sherman tank in British service

# An unquiet peace

AFTER THE AXIS DEFEAT IN 1945, the world split into two power-blocs, with the US and its allies (the West) opposing the Soviet Union and its supporters. This led to the Cold War. Direct conflict between the US and the Soviet Union did not occur, but there were regional armed clashes as the two superpowers vied to extend their influence on the world. The Cold War ended in the early 1990s with the collapse of the Soviet Union, but hidden ethnic and nationalist tensions resurfaced, resulting in new wars. Religion and competing for natural resources also helped to fuel regional conflicts.

An Israeli tank in the 1967 Yom Kippur War

### ARAB-ISRAELI CONFLICTS
The founding of Israel in 1948 provoked an unsuccessful attack by Egypt and other neighboring Arab states. Further conflicts occurred in 1956, 1967, and 1973. Much of Israel's weaponry was supplied by the West, while the Russians provided arms to the Arab nations. Today, the status of Palestinian Arabs in Israeli-controlled areas is a cause of regional tension and a key issue in world politics.

### WARS OF INDEPENDENCE
In the postwar years, liberation groups fought for independence in some African and Asian countries still ruled by Western colonial powers. Sometimes the rebels, or insurgents, had to resort to making their own weapons. Often the insurgents used ambushes (surprise attacks from hidden positions) and hit-and-run raids against their better-armed opponents.

Homemade gun used by independence fighters in Kenya against the British, 1950s

British SAS badge, bearing the motto "Who dares wins"

### SPECIAL FORCES
Special forces units, such as Britain's Special Air Service (SAS), are a key element of the modern army. These elite troops often work far behind enemy lines, carrying out reconnaissance and raids. Although they operate as small groups, their stealth, speed, and teamwork can have a significant impact.

### THE RISE OF THE HELICOPTER
Helicopters were in general military use by the 1950s, but it was during the American war in Vietnam (1964–1973) that they really proved their worth. Some helicopters carried troops into battle, and moved vehicles, stores, and ammunition over difficult terrain. Others lifted casualties out of combat zones. When armed with rockets, machine guns, and grenade-launchers, they also functioned as ground-attack aircraft.

US soldiers leap from a Bell UH1-D in the Vietnam War

*Rear sight*

*Front sight*

Russian-made AK-47

*Folding metal stock, or handle; other versions had a fixed wooden stock*

*Trigger*

*Curved magazine holds amunition*

## COLD-WAR KILLER
In 1949, the Russian Army adopted the 30-round Avtomat Kalashnikova AK-47 automatic rifle. The Russians also supplied the AK-47 to fellow Communist states and to forces they supported in the regional conflicts of the Cold War. Tough, simple to use, cheap to make, and easy to clean and maintain, the AK-47 is still in use today. In all, perhaps 50 million AK-47s have been made.

## PORTABLE ANTIAIRCRAFT MISSILES
The first antiaircraft missiles were very large and intended to defend against bombers. The development of portable missiles changed the dynamics of the battlefield. Soldiers at last had an effective weapon against enemy helicopters and low-flying jets. Insurgents, too, had great success with these missiles. In the 1980s, *mujahedin* fighters in Afghanistan used US-supplied Stinger missiles against the aircraft of the occupying Russian forces. They shot down over 250 aircraft with Stingers before the Russian Army retreated in 1989. Following the invasion of Iraq in 2003 by the US-led Coalition forces, Iraqi insurgents used similar missiles against Coalition aircraft.

## ANTIAMBUSH VEHICLE
Ambushes have long been a favorite insurgent tactic. In the early 21st century, insurgents have made increasing use of Improvised Explosive Devices (IEDs) and landmines to combine maximum damage to their opponents with little risk to themselves. Aware that high casualties can undermine the public's support for a war, armies are now equipping themselves with specially designed vehicles that can withstand the impact of mines and IEDs.

German soldier with Stinger antiaircraft missile

*Bomb-proof armored body*

*Portable communications dish*

*Dish sends signals via satellites in space*

MaxxPro antiambush vehicle, widely used by US-led Coalition forces in Iraq

*Electronics and power pack*

## BATTLEFIELD COMMUNICATIONS
Information relayed from the battlefield allows military commanders to build up a picture of enemy forces and direct their own forces to best effect. Today, electronic communications systems aided by computer and satellite technology create direct, secure links between the combat zone, headquarters, and even national capitals. They also keep individual soldiers and units in touch with one another in the midst of battle.

# Find out more

With a wealth of information available on the internet, and superb castles, forts, and museums to visit, there are plenty of opportunities to learn more about the lives of soldiers and the experience of battle. Reenactment groups using replica uniforms and weapons give a sense of living history. Battlefield tours help you to understand key conflicts. To get the most out of your visit or tour, read up about the battle beforehand, and take a tour with an official guide who can explain the terrain to you. Remember that battlefields were not a tourist spectacle to their combatants, many of whom lost their lives there.

Royal Armories, Leeds, UK

**MILITARY MUSEUMS**
Museums give a close-up view of weapons, uniforms, and equipment used throughout history, and an overview of the development of military technology. Most museums have education departments whose staff help bring artifacts to life. Notable UK museums include the Imperial War Museum and National Army Museum, London, and the Royal Armories, Leeds, which also has a base in the Frazier Museum of International History, Lexington, Kentucky.

## USEFUL WEBSITES

- The website of the US Army's Center of Military History features online exhibits and a list of military museums:
  **www.history.army.mil/**
- The About.com Military History site has a wealth of information, with summaries of more than 200 conflicts:
  **militaryhistory.about.com**
- The National World War II Museum website features historical photos and an interactive timeline:
  **www.nationalww2museum.org**
- On PBS's Civil War site, you can examine historical photos and even make your own movie:
  **www.pbs.org/civilwar/**
- Knights in Central Park presents a vitual tour of the Metropolitan Museum's outstanding arms and armor collection:
  **www.metmuseum.org/explore/knights/home.html**
- On All Fronts, a website of the Canadian Film Board, features many film clips relating to World War II:
  **www.nfb.ca/ww2/**
- America's National Parks Service maintains US battle sites. Select "by topic" on its "Find a Park" search page to locate Civil War and Revolutionary War battlefields:
  **www.nps.gov/findapark/index.htm#**
- To find the grave of a relative killed in the two world wars, see the Commonwealth War Graves Commission's website:
  **www.cwgc.org/**
- The American Battle Monuments Commission gives details of war graves for US military personnel:
  **www.abmc.gov**

Fortifications at Besançon, France

**CASTLES AND FORTS**
Defenses such as castles and forts played a key role in military strategy, and some were the scenes of long, dramatic sieges. Many of these places are open to the public, with displays to help you understand what you are seeing, and perhaps exhibits of arms and armor, too. Europe is rich in castles and fortifications. Those designed by France's Marshal Vauban (1633–1707), such as Neuf-Brisach, Besançon, and Le Quesnoy, are great examples of military engineering. In the US, Fort Ticonderoga, in New York State, and the Alamo, in Texas, are also well worth visiting.

Gettysburg battlefield, Pennsylvania

English Civil War reenactment society

## FAMILY CONNECTIONS

Most survivors of World War I have now died, and there are ever-fewer veterans of World War II, but if any of your relatives took part in these wars your family may have kept their letters, photographs, and perhaps medals. Other relatives may have served more recently in the armed forces. They may not want to discuss their combat experiences, but they may be willing to tell you about life in the military.

Military memorabilia

## REENACTMENTS

Some military history groups reenact battles on or near the sites where they were actually fought. There are good annual events at Albuera in Spain (1811) and at Waterloo in Belgium (1815). Other groups do not refight battles, but specialize in displays that give a feel for the experience of soldiers in the past.

## WAR MEMORIALS

Memorials can be found on battlefields, like those to soldiers who died on the Somme in World War I, or on home soil, such as the US Vietnam Veterans' Memorial in Washington, D.C., and the UK Armed Forces Memorial in Staffordshire, England. Some countries honor unidentified soldiers who died with a tomb to the Unknown Soldier. The UK has one in London's Westminster Abbey; the US in Arlington National Cemetery, Virginia; and Russia in the Kremlin, Moscow.

## BATTLEFIELD TOURS

American battlefields are generally well-maintained. Gettysburg in Pennsylvania (1863), the decisive battle of the Civil War, is particularly evocative. Sites tend to be less well preserved in the UK, although the 1645 battlefield of Naseby, the key clash of the English Civil War, is being made more accessible to the public. World War I battlefields in France and Belgium are widely visited, especially Ieper (Ypres), the Somme, and Verdun. So too are the beaches of Normandy, France, where Allied invasion forces landed in World War II.

Kranji War Memorial to Allied soldiers, Singapore

## Places to visit

**FORT TICONDEROGA, NEW YORK STATE**
This fort, which saw action in the Seven Years War (1756–1763) and the Revolutionary War (1775–1783), has extensive weapons and uniform collections, and also hosts reenactments.

**GETTYSBURG BATTLEFIELD, GETTYSBURG, PENNSYLVANIA**
Tour the site of the Civil War's Battle of Gettysburg, which now features a new museum.

**CALIFORNIA STATE MILITARY MUSEUM, SACRAMENTO, CALIFORNIA**
California's military museum features artifacts from the age of the conquistadors to today.

**THE METROPOLITAN MUSEUM, NEW YORK CITY**
The Met boasts one of the world's finest collections of art and armor, with objects ranging from 400 BCE to the 19th century.

**THE ALAMO, SAN ANTONIO, TEXAS**
This former mission and fortress compound was the site of a key battle between the forces of the Republic of Texas and Mexico in 1836.

**YORKTOWN BATTLEFIELD, VIRGINIA**
Take a tour with a park ranger and find out how American and French forces defeated the British to secure independence for the United States.

**NATIONAL WORLD WAR II MUSEUM, NEW ORLEANS, LOUISIANA**
Opened in 2000 as the D-Day Museum, the museum illuminates the US experience of the war.

# Glossary

**AMMUNITION** Bullets and shells fired by pistols, rifles, machine guns, and artillery.

**ANTIAIRCRAFT MISSILE** A ground-to-air missile with an explosive warhead.

Machine gun bullet

**ARCHER** A person who uses the bow for war, hunting, or target practice.

**ARMOR** Protective clothing or coverings worn in combat, usually made of fabric or metal. In the 20th century, the word became a general term for armored vehicles such as tanks.

**ARROW** A slender projectile, usually pointed at one end and feathered at the other, that is shot from a bow. Short arrows shot from crossbows are properly called bolts or quarrels.

**ARTILLERY** Large guns, such as cannons, howitzers, and mortars.

**BARRACKS** A building or group of buildings that provides permanent accommodation for military personnel.

Artillery gun at the lookout point of Oliver Hill, Western Australia

**BATTALION** An infantry unit midway in size between a company and a regiment.

**BAYONET** A bladed weapon that attaches to the muzzle of a firearm. Early bayonets were inserted into the muzzle, but these had the disadvantage of preventing the weapon from being fired when the bayonet was attached.

**BILLET** Lodgings for a soldier with local inhabitants rather than in an army camp.

**BIVOUAC** A temporary open-air army camp.

**BOW** A weapon that uses a tensioned string to shoot an arrow or bolt. Types of bow include the short bows made of horn and sinew used by eastern horse-archers; the medieval wooden longbow; and the medieval crossbow, which had a short bow fixed horizontally to a shaft.

**BREECH-LOADER** A firearm loaded from the breech (the end of the barrel nearest the user). Breech-loaders could be reloaded and fired more quickly than muzzle-loading weapons.

**BROADSWORD** A sword with a wide, heavy blade and sharp edges that is designed for slashing and cutting rather than stabbing.

**CALIBER** A measure of the inner width of a gun barrel.

**CAMOUFLAGE** Natural or man-made coverings that are used to disguise and conceal soldiers and their equipment.

**CANNON** An artillery piece that reaches maximum range when its barrel is at an angle of 45°.

**CARBINE** A short, smooth-bore or rifled firearm, often used by mounted soldiers.

**CARTRIDGE** A metal container holding a bullet and gunpowder for use in firearms. Early cartridges were made of paper.

**CASE SHOT** An iron artillery shell filled with metal balls set in a charge of gunpowder. The shell exploded in the air, showering balls down on to the target. Also called shrapnel.

**CASUALTIES** Individuals wounded, killed, taken prisoner, or reported missing in battle.

**CAVALRY** Soldiers who are trained to ride and fight on horseback.

**CHARIOT** A wheeled, horse-drawn vehicle used in combat.

**COLD WAR** The military and political tension that existed between Western nations and Soviet Russia and its allies in the aftermath of World War II.

**COLORS** The flags carried by infantry regiments. Cavalry regiments traditionally carried smaller banners, known as standards, cornets, or guidons.

**COMMISSIONED OFFICER** A military leader who is appointed by his or her head of state, and who is part of the recognized officer hierarchy. In most armies the lowest commissioned officer rank is Lieutenant and the highest is Field Marshal.

**COMMON SHELL** An iron artillery shell filled with gunpowder.

**COMPANY** For much of history, the smallest infantry unit, typically commanded by a captain. Today, there are smaller units such as platoons and squads.

**CUIRASSIER** A heavily armored cavalryman from the 17th to early 19th centuries who wore a metal *cuirass* (breastplate and backplate).

**DAGGER** A weapon with a short, pointed blade used for stabbing at close quarters.

**DRAGOON** A 17th-century infantryman who traveled on horseback, but fought mostly on foot. Dragoons eventually became a type of cavalry.

**DRILL** Repetitive training to promote discipline and instill a set response to orders.

**ENGINEER** An officer or soldier who constructs fortifications and builds or improves roads, railroads, and accommodation. Engineers also try to destroy similar enemy facilities.

**FATIGUES** Uniform worn by off-duty soldiers.

**FLINTLOCK** In firearms, a mechanism that ignited the gunpowder charge, using sparks created by striking a flint against a steel plate.

**FORTIFICATIONS** Defense works that are either permanent, such as castles and forts, or temporary, such as trenches and bunkers.

**GRAPESHOT** A container of musket balls fired from a cannon. It split up as it left the cannon, scattering the balls at approaching troops. Grapeshot caused terrible casualties when used at close range. Also called canister.

Turkish Tufenjieff grenade

**GREAVES** Metal shinguards worn by many warriors in ancient times.

**GRENADE** In the 17th and 18th centuries, gunpowder-filled ceramic or iron globes thrown by individual soldiers. The 20th century saw the introduction of rifle-grenades, which could be fired from rifles.

**GRENADIER** Originally, an infantryman who was trained to throw grenades. The term was later used more generally to refer to elite troops.

**GUNPOWDER** An explosive mixture of sulfur, saltpeter, and charcoal used to propel bullets and shells from firearms and artillery.

**HALBERD** A long-handled weapon topped by an ax-blade and a sharp point. Halberds were carried by infantry sergeants in the 18th century.

**HELIOGRAPH** A tripod-mounted mirror that was used to send signals as flashes of reflected sunlight.

Knight jousting

**HOWITZER** An artillery piece for firing shells at high angles (more than 45°). Howitzers tend to have longer barrels than mortars.

**HUSSAR** A type of light cavalryman mounted on a fast horse. Hussars typically took part in skirmishing and reconnaissance.

**INFANTRY** Soldiers who fight on foot. Infantry traditionally formed the bulk of most armies.

**INSURGENT** A fighter, typically not part of a conventional military force, who wages war against either the state or an occupying army.

**KNIGHT** A mounted and armored warrior, usually of noble birth. Knights dominated warfare for much of the Middle Ages.

**LANCE** A weapon used in mounted combat, especially by knights, with a long wooden shaft and a sharp metal head.

**LEGIONARY** A soldier of ancient Rome.

**LIGHT TROOPS** Infantry and cavalry trained to move quickly and use light weapons.

**LIMBER** A small, horse-drawn carriage for towing a cannon. The limber carried tools and ammunition for the cannon.

**LOGISTICS** The practical art of moving bodies of troops and keeping them supplied.

**MACE** A handheld weapon with a heavy metal head, often with metal spikes or flanges.

**MACHINE-GUN** A rapid-fire weapon, often of rifle caliber, with its ammunition generally contained in a fabric belt or metal magazine.

**MAGAZINE** The ammunition container attached to a rifle or machine gun.

**MATCHLOCK** A primitive form of firearm ignition, in which a smouldering cord was used to ignite the weapon's gunpowder charge.

**MORTAR** A short-barreled artillery piece used to launch explosive projectiles, properly called "bombs," at a high angle (more than 45°). Mortars were often used in sieges, because they could fire over the top of fortifications and defenses.

**MUSKET** A smooth-bore, muzzle-loading firearm that preceded the rifle.

**MUZZLE-LOADER** A firearm that is loaded by inserting the charge and projectile into its muzzle (the end farthest from the user).

**NCO** (noncommissioned officer) A soldier who ranks between a private (ordinary soldier) and a commissioned officer. NCOs are appointed from within the army, rather than by the state. Corporals and sergeants are NCOs.

**PHALANX** A closely packed body of infantry. It was the formation used by hoplite warriors in ancient Greece.

**PIKE** An infantry weapon consisting of an extremely long wooden shaft with a sharp iron tip.

**PISTOL** A firearm that can be used one-handed. Pistols were traditionally carried by cavalry and officers, and sometimes as personal protection by soldiers (such as military policemen) whose main role was not direct combat.

American Civil War saber

**POLEAX** A weapon consisting of an ax-head mounted on a long shaft.

**PRISONERS OF WAR** Soldiers captured in battle or as a result of formal surrender.

**QUADRANT** A device for measuring the firing angle of an artillery piece to calculate how far a shot would go.

**RANK** An soldier's status in the military hierarchy, usually used as a prefix to his or her name, as in Major Smith.

**RAPIER** A thin-bladed sword used for thrusting and stabbing.

**RECONNAISSANCE** Scouting and patrolling to gather details of terrain or of the enemy's strength, location, and behavior.

**REGIMENT** A military unit made up of several battalions, often with a geographical title (Middlesex Regiment) or number (22nd Regiment). The groupings above the regiment are, in increasing size: brigade, division, corps, army, and army group.

**RIFLE** A firearm with spiral grooves (rifling) on the inside of its barrel. The grooves spin the bullet or shell in flight, increasing its stability and accuracy.

**ROUND SHOT** Artillery ammunition consisting of solid balls made at first from stone, and later from iron.

**SABER** A type of heavy sword with a curving blade, used mainly by cavalry.

**SAMURAI** Members of a warrior class that enjoyed elite status in medieval Japanese society. In many ways, the samurai were the Japanese equivalent of European knights.

British colonel's rank slide, worn over the epaulette

**SAPPER** Another word for an army engineer. The word comes from the practice of "sapping," when engineers would dig zigzag trenches toward a besieged fortress.

**SIEGE** The practice of blockading a city, town, or fortress by military forces in order to capture it. If the attackers could not break through the fortifications, a lack of food and water would often force the defenders to surrender.

**SKIRMISHING** Harassing the enemy by engaging them in short battles with small groups of mobile troops.

**SMOOTH-BORE BARREL** A gun barrel with a smooth inner surface (*see* Rifle).

**SPEAR** A long shaft with a sharply pointed end, used for throwing or thrusting. Throwing spears are often called javelins.

**SPECIAL FORCES** Elite troops who carry out high-risk missions behind enemy lines.

**STRATEGIC BOMBING** The use of heavy bombing by aircraft to destroy an enemy's industrial and military capacity and to undermine the morale of its people.

**SWORD** A long-bladed weapon for cutting, slashing, or stabbing.

**TACTICS** The art of fighting battles and military engagements.

**TANK** A heavily armored combat vehicle that moves on continuous tracks, usually armed with cannons and machine guns.

**TRENCH** A man-made ditch with reinforced sides, used for protection. Trenches could be continuous, as in World War I, or one- or two-man "foxholes."

**WAR HAMMER** A handled weapon with a hammerhead on one side and a sharp spike on the other.

Automatic Colt 1911 A1 Pistol

# Index

## A

Aboriginal peoples, 37
Afghan Wars, 43
aircraft, 25
Alexander the Great, 44
ammunition, 26, 30, 42
ammunition pouches, 9, 48
Antietam, battle of, 50
Arabs, 7
armor, 11, 38, 44, 47
arrows, 36–7, 44
artillery, 26, 34–5, 50
Assyrians, 7
Austria, 55
Austro-Prussian War, 20

## B

badges, 16–17
Baker, Ezekiel, 43
Balaclava, battle of, 16
balloons, 24, 25
Bannockburn, battle of, 39
batons, 17
battalions, 14–15
battle-axes, 38–9
bayonets, 42, 43, 47
Big Elk, 56
binoculars, 25
bivouacking, 21
Boer War, 57, 59, 60
Bohun, Sir Henry de, 39
bombs, 32, 34
boomerangs, 37
Boudicca, 44
Bouvines, battle of, 38
bows and arrows, 36–7
Bradley, General Omar, 52
bravery medals, 58
breastplates, 47
bridges, 54, 55
British army, 16–17, 21, 26, 39, 43, 48, 51, 52, 58–9, 61, 63
broadswords, 40, 41
bullets, 42, 43
burgonet, 47
Burma, 49
buttons, 14

## C

callipers, 28
campaign medals, 59
cannons, 26–9, 32, 34–5, 46, 49, 50, 55
cannonballs, 26, 28, 46, 48, 49
carbines, 10, 48, 51
cartridges, 30, 42, 48
cavalry, 10–11, 13, 19, 20, 24–5, 41, 44–5, 46–8, 52
cemeteries, 63
chariots, 7
Charles V, Emperor, 45
Charles the Bold, 45
China, 16, 18
Civil War, 13, 19, 25, 30, 32, 33, 50, 51, 53, 57, 60
Clausewitz, Carl von, 6
claymore, 41
close combat, 44–5
coats of arms, 18
Coehoorn, Menno van, 32
colors, 18–19, 56
Colt revolvers, 43
communications, 52–3
companies, 14–15
compasses, 24
conscription, 8
Coote, Sir Eyre, 58
Cossacks, 20, 48
Crécy, battle of, 36, 37, 63
Crimean War, 15, 16, 20–1, 56, 60–1, 62–3
Cromwell, Oliver, 46
crossbows, 36, 37, 60
Crusades, 37, 56
cuirass, 10, 27
cuirassiers, 10–11
Custer, Major-General, 53
Cyprus, 6

## D E F

daggers, 38, 39
decorations, 58–9
defeat, 56–7
Dettingen, battle of, 49
diseases, 60–1
dragoons, 10, 48, 53
drill, 12–15, 40, 45
drums, 53
Dunant, Henry, 60
East Norfolk Regiment, 18
Edward, Black Prince, 63
Egypt, 7, 59
engineering, 54–5
enlisting, 8
ensigns, 18
epaulettes, 17
field guns, 26–9
firearms, 42–3, 46–9
Fleurus, battle of, 25
flintlocks, 43, 48
footsoldiers, 8–9
Fort Wagner, battle of, 51
fortifications, 32, 54–5
France, 7, 19, 20–1, 25, 27, 30, 36–7, 38, 42–3, 48–9, 52, 54–5, 58
Franco-Prussian War, 10, 29, 31, 41, 50
Frederick the Great, 12, 48, 62
Fuentes de Oñoro, battle of, 26

## G

Gardner gun, 50
Gatling gun, 30–1
gauntlet sword, 40
Genghis Khan, 14
George II of England, 49
Germany, 29, 31, 47, 50, 55, 58
gorget, 17
Gouvion St.-Cyr, Marshal, 14
grapeshot, 29, 30
Greece, ancient, 6, 44
grenadiers, 8, 37
guidons, 19
gunners, 26–9, 34–5, 49, 55
gunpowder, 28, 29, 46–7
guns, field, 26–9
Gustavus Adolphus of Sweden, 46

## H I J

halberds, 45
hand grenades, 36, 37
Hardee's *Tactics*, 13
harness, 11
Hegelbord, battle of, 42
heliograph, 52
helmets, 11, 38, 44
hoplon, 6
Hornby, Lady, 62
horses, 7, 10–11, 20–1, 26, 44
howitzers, 32, 33
Hundred Years War, 36, 63
hussars, 18, 25
hussif, 8
India, 20, 38, 39, 40, 52
Indian Wars, 51
infantry, 8–9, 15, 42, 44, 45, 46–8
Inkerman, battle of, 61, 62
Italy, 25, 38, 44
Japan, 16, 18, 36, 38, 40, 59, 63
javelins, 36, 44
John Sobieski of Poland, 45

## K L M N

knights, 7, 10, 12, 36, 38, 45, 56, 58
lances, 44
Lee, Robert E, 51
Lee Enfield rifles, 51
limber, 26, 27
linstock, 27, 28
Little Big Horn, battle of, 53
longbows, 36
looting, 21
Louis XIV of France, 62
maces, 38, 45
machine guns, 30–1, 50
Maratha Confederacy, 39
Matthias Corvinus of Hungary, 18
medals, 58–9, 62
medicine, 60–1
memorials, 62, 63
mitrailleuse, 30–1
Mongols, 14, 44
mortars, 32–3, 34–5
muskets, 9, 42, 46, 47, 48
Napoleon I, Emperor, 19, 49, 56, 58
Napoleonic period, 8–9, 14, 23, 43, 57
Native Americans, 17, 36, 53, 56
Netherlands, 58
Nightingale, Florence, 60
nurses, 60

## O P Q

officers, 16
orders, 58–9

pace sticks, 15
packs, 9, 22–3
Pappenheimer rapier, 41
Paré, Ambroise, 60
parrying shields, 39
Peninsular War, 21, 48, 57
periscopes, 54
phalanx, 6
Philip Augustus of France, 38
photography, 62
pigeons, carrier, 52
pikemen, 45, 46
pistols, 43, 46, 48
Pitcher, Molly, 28
Poitiers, battle of, 7, 36, 63
Poland, 45
poleaxes, 45
pom-poms, 50
portfire, 28
Portugal, 59
powder flasks, 46
prisoners, 57
Prussia, 20, 42, 48, 58

## R

railroads, 20
rank, badges, 16–17
rapiers, 40, 41
reconnaissance, 24–5
Red Cross, 60
regimental colors, 18–19, 56
regiments, 8
Revolutionary War, 24, 28
revolvers, 43
riflemen, 12–13, 23
rifles, 42, 43, 50–1
Robert the Bruce, 39
Roman army, 22, 44
Royal Fusiliers, 17
Royal North British Dragoons, 19
Russia, 20, 48, 59, 61
Russo-Japanese War, 20, 63

## S T U V

sabers, 48
sabretaches, 24
samurai, 12, 16, 36, 40, 44
sappers, 55
Scotland, 39, 41
Seti I, Pharaoh, 7
shells, 29, 32, 33, 48, 50
shields, 6, 39
shrapnel, 32
sieges, 32, 33, 37, 54, 55
Sitting Bull, 53
smoke signals, 53
Soyer, Alexis, 20
Springfield carbines, 51
supplies, 20–1
Sutherland Highlanders, 16
Switzerland, 45
sword-breakers, 40
swords, 9, 13, 40–1, 46, 47, 57
Tartaglia, Niccolo, 34
telescopes, 24, 25
Thirty Years War, 46
transportation, 20–1
trenches, 50, 52, 54, 55
trumpets, 52
Turkey, 59
uniforms, 8–9, 11, 16–17
Uxbridge, Earl of, 60
Vauban, Sébastien de, 54
Victoria, Queen, 59
victory, 56–7
volley guns, 46

## W X Y Z

wagons, 21
war hammers, 38
Waterloo, battle of, 18, 19, 27, 49, 56, 59, 60
weapons:
  field guns, 26–9
  firearms, 42–3, 46–9
  high-angle fire, 32–3
  maces and battle-axes, 38
  rapid-fire, 30–1
  rifles, 50–1
  swords, 40–1
  weapon training, 12–15
Wellington, Duke of, 24, 27, 39, 48, 56, 58
whistles, 53
William I of the Netherlands, 58
Wolfe, James, 62
women, 12, 40, 44
World War I, 20, 32, 40, 50, 52, 63
wounded soldiers, 60–1
Zulus, 16

---

# Acknowledgments

**Dorling Kindersley would like to thank:**
For their help with photography & information: 95th Rifles & Re-enactment Living History Unit (Les Handscombe, Martin Handscombe, Dennis Wraight, Nick McMillan); the Army Museums Ogilby Trust; Angels & Bermans (film costumiers); the British Museum (Nick Nicholls of the photographic service); Mark Dennis; David Edge (Histrionix Ltd) and Mark Churms, Paul Ellis, Pierre de Hugo, Anthony Perkins, Chris Seidler, & Ian Smith; Freddie Edge; the Trustees of the Florence Nightingale Museum (& Timothy Bonham-Carter); Stephen Naegel; the Museum of Artillery in the Rotunda, (Stan Walter); the Royal Green Jackets Museum (Major R.D. Cassidy); the Trustees of the National Museum of Scotland (Scottish United Services Museum); the Sulgrave Manor Board, Northamptonshire; the Trustees of the Wallace Collection, London. For additional photography: Peter Chadwick: pp. 30-31, 33, 49, 50. For design & editorial help: Mark Haygarth, Joseph Hoyle, Susan St. Louis, Gin von Noorden. For the index: Hilary Bird.

For this edition, the publisher would also like to thank: author Richard Holmes for assisting with the updates; Lisa Stock for editorial assistance; David Ekholm-JAlbum, Sunita Gahir, Susan St Louis, Steve Setford, Lisa Stock & Bulent Yusuf for the clip art; Sue Nicholson & Ted Kinsey for the wall chart; Monica Byles & Stewart J Wild for proofreading; Margaret Parrish & John Searcy for Americanization.

**Picture credits**
The publisher would like to thank the following for their kind permission to reproduce their photographs:
(Key: a-above; b-below/bottom; c-center; f-far; l-left; r-right; t-top)
**Ancient Art and Architecture Collection:** 14ar, 37ar, 56al. **akg-images:** 64bc. **Alamy Images:** Jon Arnold Images Ltd 68cr; Dennis MacDonald 68-69b. **The Board of Trustees of the Armouries:** 68tr. **Bridgeman Art Library:** Bibliothèque des arts décoratifs: 33cr, 43ar; Bibliothèque nationale, Paris: 36bl; British Library: 45br, 49al, 54ar; Jean-Loup Charmet: 32al, 32cr, 32cl, 33bcr, 37bcl, 46ar; Imperial War Museum, London (I Want you for the U. S. Army by James Montgomery Flagg, 1917): 8ar; John Spink Fine Watercolours, London: 9br; Private Collection: 38br. **Corbis:** Bettmann 66b; Henri Bureau / Sygma 66tr; Randy Faris 64-65, 66-67, 68-69, 70-71(background). **DK Images:** The Board of Trustees of the Armouries 67t; Gettysburg National Military Park, PA 71crb; Imperial War Museum 64cl, 70crb, 71tr; Judith Miller / Wallis & Wallis 69tr; Museum of the Regiments, Calgary 64-65b; Rough Guides 69c; Lieutenant Commander W.M. Thornton MBE RD RNR 64cr. **E.T. Archive:** 16ar, 20cl, 21al, 24acl, 26bl, 36br, 44al, 52bl, 53al, 56br, 57bc; Bibliothèque nationale, Paris: 7cl; Musée Malmaison: 49ar; Museum der Stadt, Wien: 55al; Parker Gallery: 26br. **Fitzwilliam Museum, University of Cambridge:** 16cr. **Michael Holford:** 7ar, 15al. **Hulton-Deutsch Collection:** 8al, 26bcr, 27bl, 28br, 30al, 34br, 34bl, 56ar. **Imperial War Museum:** 66ca. **Mansell Collection:** 20cr, 36al, 36ar, 42bc. **Mary Evans Picture Library:** 12al, 13cr, 14cr, 15ar, 18br, 20bc, 25ar, 29cr, 31ar, 39acr, 41al, 42ar, 44cl, 46al, 50cl, 52ar, 54bc, 55bl, 60al, 60cl, 61al, 62bl, 63ar; Explorer Archives: 20al. **Musée de l'Armée, Paris:** 18al, 18-19a, 27br, 44ar. **© National Army Museum, London** - photograph supplied by Bridgeman Art Library: 16br. **PA Photos:** DPA 67cra; Haraz N. Ghanbari / AP 67clb. **Peter Newark's Military Pictures:** 10al, 19cr, 31br, 35al, 43al, 46bl, 51acl, 51bcr, 51bl, 53ac, 54acl, 56bl, 57tc, 58ar, 63tc. **Range / Bettmann:** 50al. **Robert Harding Picture Library:** 63cr; Musée de l'Armée: 55ar. **Trustees of the Royal Hussars Museum:** 25bcr. **Shutterstock:** Ovidiu Lordachi 67br; Stephen Mulcahey 69tl. **Science Museum / Science & Society Picture Library:** 25al. **Mr. A.D. Theobald, courtesy of the Royal Signals Museum:** 52al. **TopFoto.co.uk:** 64tr, 65tr. **Jo Walton:** 66cl.

**Wall chart: The Bridgeman Art Library:** John Spink Fine Watercolours, London, UK cl; **DK Images:** The 95th Rifles and Re-enactment Living History Unit cra, crb (trumpet); Gettysburg National Military Park, PA bl; Royal Green Jackets Museum, Winchester bc, clb (Spanish rapier), cr (sketch and telescope), fcra; Wallace Collection, London fclb (war hammer and mace).

**Jacket:** *Front:* **The Art Archive:** Gunshots cla; Musée Condé Chantilly/Gianni Dagli Orti b; **DK Images:** Geoff Dann © Dorling Kindersley, Courtesy of David Edge ftl, Dave King © Dorling Kindersley, Courtesy of the Ermine Street Guard tr; Peter Chadwick © Museum of Artillery, The Rotunda, Woolwich, London cra; Dave King © Dorling Kindersley, Courtesy of Warwick Castle, Warwick ftr. *Back:* **Corbis:** Bettmann br; **DK Images:** Courtesy of Andrew L Chernack tc; Geoff Brightling © Dorling Kindersley, Courtesy of the 95th Rifles & Re-enactment Living History Unit cra; Geoff Dann © The Wallace Collection, London cb, crb (mace)

All other images © Dorling Kindersley
For further information see:
www.dkimages.com